HARVARD EAST ASIAN MONOGRAPHS

5

_____

RANDOM NOTES ON RED CHINA

1936-1945

RANDOM NOTES ON RED CHINA

1936–1945

by

Edgar Snow

Published by the
East Asian Research Center
Harvard University

Distributed by
Harvard University Press
Cambridge, Mass.
1974

The East Asian Research Center (formerly Chinese Economic
and Political Studies) at Harvard University administers
research projects designed to further scholarly understanding
of China, Korea, Japan, and adjacent areas. These studies
have been assisted by grants from the Ford Foundation.

Library of Congress No. 58-146
SBN 674-74900-6

Data on the early years of the Chinese Communist movement, particularly on its decade in the wilderness between the Kuomintang-Comintern split of 1927 and the United Front of 1937, is all too scarce. As a rebel movement on the defensive, proscribed and under severe pressure from the Nationalist Government of China, it left rather little written record during those years. Aside from official Communist accounts produced in retrospect and subject to distortion accordingly, historians have to rely more than usual on the reports of observers, particularly of journalists who collected information from Communist leaders themselves when opportunity was particularly favorable in the mid-thirties.

Among all the reporters of that era, Edgar Snow was outstanding. The publication of his Red Star Over China in 1938 was in itself an event in modern Chinese history. The book was colorful reading, illustrated with the author's own photographs of the actors in the story. It gave a human and detailed account of what then seemed to be an under-dog, Robin Hood type of movement among a remote and mysterious but likeable people. It was widely read by an American public for whom Nazi Germany in the West and militarist Japan in the East had already become great and mortal enemies -- in the days before communist totalitarianism, West and East, had succeeded to that position.

Red Star Over China depicted a revolutionary movement which stoutly maintained its dyed-in-the-wool communism but which was then confined to a purely agrarian base in a distant and arid region. It had just escaped annihilation in Kiangsi, suffered the attrition of the Long March, and entered with the Comintern on a united front policy of temporary moderation, reform and patriotic collaboration against the national enemy. When Snow got his story, in the summer and early fall of 1936, the communist headquarters were still at Pao-an in northern Shensi, Yenan having not yet been occupied. This was an auspicious moment to record the adventurous story of Red China, when its often bloody exploits could be recollected in momentary tranquility.

By 1936 Edgar Snow had already spent seven years in China as a journalist. His first book, Far Eastern Front, had described Japan's aggression in Manchuria and North China and at Shanghai. Teaching journalism at Yenching University in 1934-35, he had studied modern Chinese literature and been a first-hand observer of student life and thought. By the time opportunity offered to visit the new Red area in June 1936, he had prepared himself by years of professional work not only to score a journalistic scoop but also to make a contribution to the Chinese historical record. Red Star Over China still contains the major biography of Mao Tse-tung (pages 111-67 of the first edition). Nearly every one of its 450 pages records data of more or less historical value, on the major aspects of the preceding fifteen years of Chinese communism. Here was a case where a well-prepared and able reporter succeeded in seizing a unique historical opportunity.

Finding in 1956 that Mr. Snow still had in his files data he had recorded in his notebooks twenty years before but never used, we urged him to transcribe portions of it for publication as an aid to research. This volume is the result, produced simply and for the scholar rather than for the general public. We are indebted to Mr. Snow for his readiness to add these further notes to the scanty first-hand reports available on an important and formative period.

Some of the items now published for the first time in this volume, such as those giving data on the Red Army in the Long March, were collected at the time Mr. Snow was preparing the manuscript of Red Star Over China. The biographical information similarly is part of an active journalist's unused surplus of materials. Other items, such as the notes on a conversation with F.D.R., were collected in later years but have not been published heretofore or have been used only fragmentarily. The contemporary statements recorded on the Sian incident, with which the collectio. opens support a heterodox and very interesting view of the Moscow-Yenan relationship in that famous crisis.

J.K. Fairbank

Cambridge, Mass.
September 1957

AUTHOR'S PREFACE

"Travel, in the younger sort, is a part of education; in the elder a part of experience," said Mr. Bacon. "He that travelleth into a country before he hath entrance into the language, goeth to school, and not to travel."

The epigram is, like all good epigrams, an exaggeration, for the terms cannot be so sharply separated. But if we accept its modicum of truth then I might say that my own visit among the Chinese Communists at Sian in 1936 (the year with which this small volume is mainly concerned) was about halfway between education and experience and halfway between school and travel. I was then thirty--too aged to be "the younger sort" and yet not ancient enough to called "elder"--and although I had "some entrance" into Chinese it was not enough for me to do a professional job without help.

Through the aid of Mme Sun Yat-sen I made contacts with the Chinese Communists who arranged for my trip by underground ways into the Northwest territory held by the Red Army in June 1936. I was told that I would find an interpreter at the Soviet "capital" (Pao-an) but that it would be well to bring in someone on my own. I sent to Peking for a young Chinese writer to join me and he arrived before I left Sian but at the last minute changed his mind and would not go. I therefore had to leave without an interpreter but I wrote my wife to ask her to try to get one of two Yenching University student friends to follow me. Wang Ju-mei (who later joined the Communist party and took the name Huang Hua) was the one who accepted. He eventually caught up with me after I had reached the Western "front" in Kansu.

The first English-speaking Chinese I encountered after entering the Red areas was Chou En-lai, who was in command of the Eastern "front," whom I described in Red Star Over China and who reappears in these pages. He supplied me with an armed escort and I proceeded to Pao-an, where I met Mao Tse-tung and where there were several English-speaking Communists. Among them was Wu Liang-p'ing (see page 47), who was assigned to me as an interpreter in my official interviews. He could not accompany me on my travels to the West, however, and I was without an interpreter until Wang Ju-mei joined me. I returned to Pao-an without any interpreter and I also had none during my week on the "road back" described toward the end of this work.

Wu Liang-p'ing interpreted for all my formal interviews with Mao Tse-tung and with other important officials at Pao-an who did not speak English. Mao asked me to write up everything he said in full, in English. The result was translated back into Chinese by Wu and Mao then amended, amplified and edited it, as I sat with him and Wu and wrote the final version. In the case of the interview with Chou En-lai which appears in these pages (for the first time), I wrote up the story, correcting Chou's English (which was very rusty), and then read it back to him and further edited it. Otherwise, as a rule I simply took down what people told me word for word except for clarifying or correcting the interpreter's syntax as we went along.

As there was only sporadic border fighting going on during most of my four months in the Northwest, and a lull in political activity while the leaders awaited the arrival of the Second Front Army from Szechwan to thrash out new questions of policy, I found little difficulty in arranging to interview anybody I wished to see. Once given the word to open up, they all welcomed the opportunity to speak to someone from the outside world for the first time in years.

Every word then was fresh and informative—even crude propaganda—and I wrote down nearly everything I heard and was often busy with pen or pencil from early morning till after midnight. Mao Tse-tung spoke to me nearly every night for several weeks, usually starting after supper at about nine or ten and often continuing until I fell asleep at two or three A. M.

During the day I always carried one or two pocket notebooks in which I scratched comments made on the fly. For regular interview appointments I had larger books, which I also used for a daily journal in which I sometimes wrote up, at greater length, observations made during the day. I have indexed sixteen books which run from fifty to one hundred-odd pages each, often written in fine hand and on both sides of the paper—for writing paper was a scarce commodity there. When a name seemed important or a word was in doubt I would ask the speaker or interpreter to write it for me in Chinese. (Later I regretted that I had not done so more often.)

In addition to my notebooks I collected other information as a result of requests I wrote out for Po Ku, Wu Liang-p'ing, Li Chiang-lin, Lu Ting-yi and others. On my return to Peking I had most of this material translated and used it or filed it away. One side project on which I embarked was a history of the Long March, for which the Red Army collected dozens of contributions for me. I have since added to these stories and it is one of my ambitions some day to attempt a book about that epic.

In the present monograph all biographical material was recorded as told to me by the principals, unless otherwise stated. Comment enclosed in parentheses was, with exceptions noted, recorded at the time of the interviews as information elicited ad lib and not necessarily relevant to the immediate line of questioning. In a few instances I added parenthetical remarks of my own while interviewing. The indented single-spaced material consists of information or comment added by me at this writing. I submitted my recollections of the Roosevelt conversations to Mrs. Roosevelt, to ask her to correct anything she felt contradicted her own knowledge or impressions of her husband's views on these subjects. She was kind enough to reply saying that she saw "nothing to correct." As for the travel notes, they were based on my own observations and direct conversations with soldiers and peasants and written up quite fully in the long hours of waiting between stages.

At no time did the Communists attempt to examine my notes or censor them. Chou En-lai's request that I not print his remarks about Chiang Kai-shek was the only case of the kind I can recall. I was asked not to reveal information of military value "to the enemy" and I of course was told a few things in confidence which I kept. Once or twice Mao Tse-tung asked me to write up his interviews while I was in their areas. I contended that my editors* and the public would not believe anything coming to them in that way, and said that all my reporting would have to be done after I had returned to Peking. Mao conceded the logic of my point and did not press the matter.

Undoubtedly I missed many opportunities to acquire information of value due to my own ignorance. I had read everything I could find about the Communists before I ventured into their territory, but it was extremely fragmentary, inaccurate and unreliable. I knew little more than the names of top political and military leaders and the history of Communist-Kuomintang relations and the civil war as seen from the outside. It took me some time

---

*Of the New York Sun and the London Daily Herald. The Sun did not use my reports of this trip; the Herald did.

to learn who was who and put the pieces together, a task in which Mao Tse-tung himself was the greatest help, so that by the time I left Pao-an to meet the army I was relatively well "informed."

With regard to the "New Data on Sian" I am sorry that it seems best to preserve the anonymity of "X" even though twenty years have elapsed, because I still lack authorization to do otherwise although I am confident that the individual would no longer object to opening these facts to the historian. My reason for publishing all this material is not, incidentally, that I think Mr. Miao's version of the aftermath of Sian was necessarily correct or the Communists necessarily wrong in the course they pursued, but simply that it has valid relevance along with other information. Here and there remarks also seem especially revelatory of Chinese Communist thinking of the time. For example, P'eng Teh-huai's comment, "You have to take a curve. You can't go directly at a thing."

In the text I have made no systematic attempt to evaluate the Sian data, but here I may offer at least a few random comments about its possible significance for what they may be worth to historians interested in that major turning-point episode in China's destiny.

It now seems probable that the Communists had encouraged Chang Hsüeh-liang to detain the Generalissimo. Their chief delegate at the Young Marshal's headquarters in Sian (Liu Ting) was in closest touch with the young officers who led the coup. The Politburo at first meant to exploit it as a means of setting up a national anti-Japanese government in Sian, isolating if not totally discrediting Chiang Kai-shek, their chief internal enemy. Moscow's sudden intervention undercut previous plans and left Mao momentarily without a clear line of support to offer Chang Hsüeh-liang. Pravda's shattering denunciation of Chang as a traitor and Japanese agent enormously weakened the Chinese Communists in their relations with him, and threw them into confusion. This vacillation and let-down in a quarter where Chang had expected help and understanding must have influenced the Young Marshal to make his independent decision to release the Generalissimo "prematurely" (see Po Ku's comment) and before the Chinese Politburo could "take a curve" to reconcile Moscow's directive with their own prior expectations and their really desperate need for minimum guarantees of political and physical survival--i.e., to use Chiang's arrest to eliminate him and divide those who wished to renew efforts to destroy them.

Following Chiang's release the Communists were in fact soon again placed at his mercy and left with no choice--having lost their chance to unite with the Tungpei and Hsipei armies--but to try by propaganda means to break out of their isolation onto the national scene. But by June 1937 Chiang Kai-shek had scattered and demoralized the once-powerful Tungpei Army, moved his own forces into Shensi, and again was blockading the Reds. The situation was bound to remind the Reds of their earlier mistakes in rejecting an all-out alliance with the Nineteenth Route Army during the Fukien Rebellion, in 1932. Once more they now seemed to face the choice of total surrender or encirclement and disaster, or retreat to the northern desert. In the same month (June) I received a letter from Mao Tse-tung (in answer to questions I had sent privately to ask what guarantee they had against this fate) in which he spoke ambiguously of the crisis in the United Front and expressed "anxiety and dissatisfaction" with the Kuomintang policy apparently aimed at all preparations for a renewal of warfare in the Northwest.

Chang Hsüeh-liang had "saved" the Communists once. Now a second stroke of luck opened up the broadest and most fertile opportunities for them. For it was in the following month that they were extricated from their precarious position only by Japan's "providential" major invasion of China, which gave Chiang no choice but to shelve any and all plans for another annihilation drive. It is unlikely that Mao failed to learn from this bitter experience or that it did not strengthen what tendency toward independence of decision the Chinese party later exhibited, particularly when it embarked on the final struggle for power.

Professor John K. Fairbank is the magician who has brought this long dormant material to life again. The compilation was begun at his suggestion and without his encouragement would doubtless not have seen print. I am also grateful to the rest of the executive committee of the Chinese Economic and Political Studies program, as well as to O. Edmund Clubb, for their help in reading the manuscript and for valuable comments. Dr. K. C. Chao has painstakingly checked the Chinese characters and supplied them for proper names throughout, while Dr. T. T. Chow has kindly contributed the fine example of his calligraphy for the cover. I am likewise indebted to Mrs. Elizabeth Matheson and Mrs. Nien-ling Leung for the surprising amount of hard labor involved in a production of this kind.

Finally, I do not forget the kindness of strangers "on the other side of the river" who made my original enterprise possible.

Edgar Snow

Palisades, New York
September 1957

CONTENTS

Appendix: Biographies in Brief

I. NEW DATA ON THE SIAN INCIDENT

1. A Postcard from Pao-an

Soon after the Generalissimo was arrested and held prisoner by Chang Hsüeh-liang 張學良 , at Sian, in December 1936, I received a postcard from Pao-an, Shensi, which had been posted at Yenan. It reached me at Peking through the regular mail and was written by a certain doctor whose name I still have no permission to reveal. He was later to become prominent in the work of the International Peace Hospitals during the Sino-Japanese war. In his card he wrote vividly and excitedly of a mass celebration held in Pao-an the night after news was received that Chiang had been arrested in Sian.

The doctor's message said that at the huge meeting addressed by Mao Tse-tung and others, a resolution was passed to demand a "mass trial" of Chiang Kai-shek as a traitor, and there was wild jubilation in the town. I no longer have the card, but I think it reached me while the Generalissimo was still being detained or had only just been released. I remember being puzzled by its tone, which indicated that the Communists had planned to hold Chiang Kai-shek a prisoner and bring him to trial and disgrace. By the time I received the card it was already plain that the Communists had changed their policy; they had declared their willingness to support his leadership in a wartime coalition of anti-Japanese forces.

However, I learned nothing more concrete to explain this contradiction until I saw X.

2. A Talk with "X"

November 2, 1937. (I quote from diary notes made the day after I saw X in Shanghai, on November 2, 1937.) During the Sian Incident H.H. Kung came to see X. He asked X to sign a statement denouncing Chang Hsüeh-liang for seizing the Generalissimo. X flatly refused to do so. Flabbergasted, Kung demanded to know why.

"What he did was right," X said. "I would have done the same thing if I had been in his place. Only I would have gone farther."

"For this," X said to me, "I have never been forgiven by them."

X knew in advance, X said, that Chang Hsüeh-liang planned something of the kind. X had even urged him to do so. "You must do something to wipe out your disgrace [loss of Manchuria at the time of his personal demoralization]," X told him. Chang was X's neighbor in Shanghai; that is, their houses in the French concession were in the same block. Hence X rejoiced at the news of

Chang's action against the Generalissimo and was depressed by his release. X was not the only one.

"Mao Tse-tung," X said, "flew into a rage when the order came from Moscow to release Chiang. Mao swore and stamped his feet. Until then they had planned to give Chiang a public trial and to organize a Northwest anti-Japanese defense government."

Chiang refused to see any Communists in Sian until Mme Chiang arrived, according to X. Chou (En-lai) went to Mme Chiang and begged her to arrange an interview with Chiang. She finally agreed. Chou was very apologetic all the time he talked to Chiang.

> At this time or a little later I learned that X had forwarded the telegram from Stalin to Mao which stated that unless the Chinese Communists used their influence to release Chiang they would be denounced by Moscow as "bandits" and repudiated before the world. It was apparently the first direct communication of the kind sent from Moscow for some time.

3. Moscow's "Mistake" about Chang Hsüeh-liang

> Following a meeting with Wang Ping-nan and his German wife, Anna, I was reminded of a conversation I had had with a certain Mr. Ku whose ming-tzu (given name) I cannot now recall, and whom I had first met in Tientsin and later saw in Shanghai. He had been a Communist for about ten years and had risen to the head of the provincial committee. He was emphatically opposed to the party's decision about Chiang Kai-shek and believed Moscow had made a mistake.

> The indented material below is added at this writing for explanatory purposes.

February 5, 1938. Ku thought that if Chiang had been kept in Sian longer it would have resulted in some real and fundamental changes in Nanking: the formation of a coalition government without civil war. As long as Chiang was held, the civil war (had it continued) could have been stopped at any time by his release. Especially after Mme Chiang, T.V. (Soong), and W.H. Donald were in Sian, it was the "chance of a decade." Ku had been in Shanghai when the order from Moscow arrived. It was worded in peremptory style (Ku said), like this: "Free Chiang at once or we will break all connections with you." The party was dumbfounded; Ku in violent disagreement; X also. The Reds had hoped to get Chiang into their areas to hold a public trial there. The change in their party line was made after Moscow's demand left them no

choice. What is remarkable is that they were able to force through the
(revised) decision without a mutiny in their armies.

"We didn't sleep for a week, trying to decide," Chou En-lai told
Ping-nan (Wang). "It was the most difficult decision of our whole lives."

Why the order? That it came from Stalin there is little doubt. Did
he already have some understanding with Chiang (re the Japanese)? Had he
been misinformed by Bogomoloff (by 1938 in disgrace) about the real situation
in the Northwest between Chiang and Chang? Chang Hsüeh-liang then had a
representative of his own in Moscow, a friend of Anna Wang; he tried in vain
(said Anna) to see the Central Committee and ask them to withhold judgment
against Chang Hsüeh-liang until they could get more reliable news. They
could not have understood the situation, thought Anna.

> Yet there was no reason why the Kremlin should have misunderstood
> the situation, even assuming that it had not been receiving detailed
> reports on developments in the Northwest from the Chinese Communists
> themselves. Following my return from Yenan in 1936 I sold Tass, in
> Peking, a complete set of all the articles I wrote for the New York
> Sun and the Daily Herald. I also told the head of Tass agency in
> Peking, off the record, exactly how the Reds were being helped by
> Chang Hsüeh-liang. Our conversation indicated that he was not
> entirely informed about that. But he himself had no doubt that Chang
> Hsüeh-liang was sincerely anti-Japanese and that his seizure of
> Chiang Kai-shek had the full support of the Chinese Communists. He
> was as astounded by the Moscow press reaction as I was. He kept
> repeating, "I don't understand. They have read all my reports. How
> could they make this mistake?"

> I had also told Colonel Lapin, the Russian military attaché, most of
> the story--as I had likewise given the full background on Sian, as I
> knew it, to Colonel Stilwell, the American military attaché. I made
> the Russian ambassador, Bogomoloff, equally well aware that the charges
> made by Moscow against Chang were a cock-and-bull story. He knew it
> and was too embarrassed to discuss it.

> I have not much doubt that Bogomoloff and Lapin did send all they knew
> to Moscow about the Sian situation, both before and after the incident,
> I am reasonably sure that Tass also sent my articles to Moscow. Not
> one was ever printed. Much later a bowdlerized version of Red Star
> Over China was published there, without my knowledge, in which all
> reference to Sian, the Comintern, Russia, and any and all "controversial"
> matters was omitted.

> "Izvestia and Pravda," I wrote, "went so far in their official dis-
> claimers of responsibility, denunciations of Chang Hsüeh-liang, and
> hosannas to Chiang Kai-shek, that they invented a story showing that
> the Sian affair was jointly inspired by the former Chinese premier,
> Wang Ching-wei 汪精衛 , and the 'Japanese imperialists'--a libel

so antipodal to the facts that even the most reactionary press in China had not dared to suggest it out of fear of ridicule. 'Prevarication is permissible, gentlemen,' it was Lenin who exclaimed, 'but within limits!'"--Red Star Over China (Random House, 1937), 410.

Bogomoloff and Lapin were both arrested in the 1937-38 purge trials and ended in disgrace or exile and possible death. I do not know the fate of the Tass correspondent. He was recalled in 1937. I never heard of him when I worked in Russia, nor ever again in any other country.

This was one of the personal experiences which would convince me that as long as Russia made Comintern policy it would always and everywhere be made first of all in the strategic interest of the U.S.S.R., as the Kremlin saw it--or, more baldly, Soviet Russian communism first, and international communism second. But of course the Stalinist true-believer never could admit the existence of any such contradiction. There is little doubt that Stalin was interested in saving Chiang Kai-shek out of fear that the Kuomintang generals, without Chiang, would in rage turn and join the Japanese in an anti-Russian pact. General Hurley reported to the State Department after a wartime conversation with Molotov in Moscow that the latter had said: "Due to the political and moral support of the Soviet government, Chiang had been allowed to return to the seat of his government and the revolutionary leader (Chang Hsüeh-liang) had been arrested."--United States Relations with China (Washington, 1949), 72.

Anna Wang told me that in the spring of 1936, when she and her husband Wang Ping-nan came through Moscow, the latter called on Wang Ming 王明 [pseudonym of Ch'en Shao-yü 陳紹禹]. They talked for days about the political situation in the Northwest. Wang Ping-nan (a nephew or kind of adopted son of Yang Hu-ch'eng 楊虎城 , then (Nationalist) pacification commissioner of the Northwest) agreed to try to persuade Yang, on his return to Sian, to join the United Front. Ping-nan was to send a wire to Wang Ming, who would then delegate a Comintern representative to call on Yang and make a connection. On his arrival in Sian, Wang anticipated trouble in persuading Yang; to his surprise Yang raised few objections. After a week's conversation about the international political situation General Yang agreed to meet the Comintern representative. Wang Ping-nan immediately (April or May) wired Wang Ming in Moscow to send his delegate. Nothing happened. He sent message after message. There was never a reply. Months and months elapsed. Yang Hu-ch'eng finally made his own contact with the Reds in Sian itself, entirely independent of Wang Ming, chief of the Chinese Communist Party (CCP) delegation in Moscow.

Only during and after the Sian Incident did the Reds enlarge their conception of the United Front from the "Northwest anti-Japanese government" to cooperation with Nanking. Until then they had hoped to split Nanking by their unity in the Northwest (with the Tung-pei, Hsi-pei and other potential defectors among the northern armies).

The significance of the comment on Wang Ming is simply that on his return from Moscow he did not, as he had expected, take his place as a leading, if not the leading member of the Chinese Politburo. One of the reasons commonly given for this was his failure to keep Moscow correctly informed on internal political conditions in China. He was rumored to be responsible for the Moscow telegram. Personally I doubt that; there were other reasons for Mao and the inner circle to keep Wang Ming from regaining prominence. But his identification with the unpopular Moscow telegram was probably an important factor in his decline.

It is also my impression that the Sian Incident was the last occasion on which Stalin issued a direct order affecting a critical decision in Chinese party policy.

4. The Story of Miao Feng-hsia 苗鳳夏 (?) (Miao Chien-ch'iu 苗劍秋)

Following is the greater part of an unpublished interview with Miao Feng-hsia, a fanatical Manchurian patriot who was political advisor to Marshal Chang Hsüeh-liang and was also his warm friend and admirer. He was a dominating influence on Sun Ming-chiu 孫銘九 , commander of the Young Marshal's bodyguard. It was Sun who actually carried out the arrest and bodily seizure of Chiang Kai-shek. Miao had intended this action to lead to still greater things, as becomes evident from the text, but the Communists did not fulfill their promises to him, he believed.

Till today Miao remains loyal to Chang; at last report he was living in exile in Tokyo. He was still trying to secure the Young Marshal's release in Formosa, where Chiang Kai-shek holds him prisoner. At the time of this interview Miao was thirty-six years old.

All parenthetical remarks below are mine.

September 13, 1938. Hongkong. "One month before the Sian Incident," said Miao, "I wrote a letter to Chang advocating the detention of Chiang Kai-shek for the purpose of organizing the nation to resist Japan, to bring about a cessation of civil war, and to form a United Front government. I thought that the expression 'People's Front' was too bolshevist. By lien-ho chan-hsien 聯合戰線 (united front) I meant that no one party would have a monopoly of leadership; there would be a genuine coalition.

"Chang Hsüeh-liang replied to me that he was (1) not strong enough to lead such an action, (2) not that ambitious, and (3) convinced he could persuade the Generalissimo to change by other methods. My idea was to begin by the organization of an anti-Japanese government in Sian. Chang's idea was to avoid an incident but to use ping-chien 兵諫 (military persuasion). After our discussion I left Sian as a result of pressure from the Blue Shirts (Chiang Kai-shek's so-called Gestapo).

"On October 22, the second day of Chiang's first visit to Sian (after Chang Hsüeh-liang became bandit-suppression commissioner), Chiang Kai-shek made a speech, saying: 'Don't speak of fighting Japan. Don't talk about the Japanese menace now. Anybody who speaks of fighting Japan now and not the Communists is not a Chinese soldier. The Japanese are far away. The Communists are right here.' That night I wrote my letter to Chang calling for Chiang's detention. The next day I made a speech at Wang-ch'i (near Sian) before the students (Manchurian cadets) and asked them, 'Why didn't you kill such a man (as Chiang)?' I wept and said, 'We are all from Tung-pei (Manchuria). We must go back to our homes. We can't be traitors and slaves.' Most of the four hundred cried. I said: 'Crying is no use. We must fight. We can fight anywhere we meet pro-Japanese forces. Why did we permit Marshal Chiang to come here and not kill him?'

"Chou En-lai and Chang Hsüeh-liang met in Fushih (Yenan) in June or July, 1936. They talked for two hours. Chang wanted to "yung-Chiang k'ang-Jih" 用蔣抗日 (use Chiang to fight Japan) while Chou wanted to "tao-Chiang k'ang-Jih" 倒蔣抗日 (overthrow Chiang to fight Japan). Chang persuaded Chou to try his way and Chou and Chang both wept. Chou said, 'We are patriots; we want to fight to save China.'"

Miao was forced into exile after his speech before the students. He went to Japan in 1936--but when the Sian Incident occurred he rushed back. He did not arrive until December 28, after Chang Hsüeh-liang had flown to Nanking and voluntarily submitted himself to Chiang Kai-shek for punishment.

"When I returned to Sian I found everything wrong. At first Chou En-lai welcomed me. He said, 'You are so pure and so brave,' and so forth. Then I asked, 'Can you be sure Chang Hsüeh-liang will return?' He answered, 'I am sure he will come back soon.' As days went on I knew Chang would not return and I again discussed the question with Chou on December 30.

"Colonel Sun Ming-chiu and Mr. Ying also doubted that the Young Marshal would be released. From this time they did not believe Chou En-lai. Chou said that if they used force there would be a long civil war as in Spain. 'You don't want to make China into another Spain do you?'

"I said: 'The Northeastern Army is very anxious about Chang Hsüeh-liang and wants him to return. If he comes back the Tung-pei and Hsi-pei (Northwestern Army, of Yang Hu-ch'eng) and Red Army can cooperate as the main anti-Japanese power. If not, they cannot cooperate.'

"Chou said: 'You must remember your national spirit now.'

"I said: 'If civil war (between Sian and Nanking) breaks out it won't be a long war. The Central Army won't fight. Their anti-Japanese feeling is too strong.'

"Chou said: 'Chiang is a hard man. It is difficult to change him.'

"I said: 'Chiang is a wavering man. If our spirit is high in Ch'ang-an (Sian), then Chiang will send the Young Marshal back to us. We can start right here the United Front for the whole country.' Chou didn't agree.

"In the middle of January P'an Han-nien 潘漢年 arrived in Sian from Nanking (as an emissary). We suspected him and arrested him as an 'unknown.' On him we found documents concerning direct Kuomintang-Communist negotiations concerning the formation of the Red district into a special area, payment of Red soldiers, existence of the Communist party, and so forth. These letters and documents were from General Chang Ch'ün 張羣 concerning negotiations with the Communist party.

"I confronted Chou En-lai with this information and asked him why he was betraying our 'Three-in-One' agreement. (Northeast-Northwest-Red Army coalition, announced as the basis of an anti-Japanese national patriotic movement at the time of Chiang's arrest.) 'Why do you negotiate separately?' I asked him. Chou turned pale when I told him what we had learned (from P'an). 'Is that why you agreed to let Chang go to Nanking? What kind of United Front is this? Who can be a friend of the Red Army now? This is not only bad for the national situation but bad for social revolution, bad for you. If you can't keep the United Front at Sian how can you keep it over the whole of China? When can China fight Japan? (Etc.)'

"I talked with Chou for six hours (insisting that Chang Hsüeh-liang must be released before any negotiations) but we did not agree. I said, 'You are too old. You are a damned fool.'

"But on the twenty-eighth (January) Chou came and said I was right. He asked for four trucks. (Chou and Po Ku 博古 and the Red delegation were guests in Sian and dependent on the Tung-pei Army for everything.) He and Po Ku and Liu Ting 劉鼎 (?) went to San-yuan (P'eng Teh-huai's 彭德懷 headquarters, nearest Red outpost). They asked me to wait for an answer. I didn't sleep that night. The next morning (January 30) I received a telegram from them at 4:00 A.M. It said: 'We have decided. Live or die together.' At 9:00 A.M. they came back into town and joyously shook hands all around. Chou and Po Ku said, 'You are right.'

"Now at that time Wang I-che 王以哲 , Ho Chu-kuo 何柱國 and Yü Hsüeh-chung 于學忠 (the most important Tung-pei generals) did not really like the alliance with the Reds. They had been pleased when they discovered that Chou was negotiating separately with Nanking. (It gave them an excuse for a break.) When Chou and Po Ku came back with their new plan, calling for insistence upon the release of Chang Hsüeh-liang before negotiations, and for use of force if necessary, they failed to get the support of Wang, Ho and Yü. Chou then said he could not help the situation."

As the firebrand leader of the younger Tung-pei officers--who had engineered the kidnapping and mutiny against the wishes of the older generals, but with Chang Hsüeh-liang's leadership--Miao had it within his power to lead another mutiny, this time to overthrow the older or senior generals.

"On the thirty-first, Sun (Colonel Sun Ming-chiu, commander of Chang Hsüeh-liang's bodyguard, who had carried out the arrest of Chiang and was Miao's first military arm) and Ying (another leader of the young officers) sent a car for me and wanted me to attend a meeting. I refused to go; they planned to organize support for the elimination of Wang, Ho and Yü. Because I did not attend they did not come to a decision. About fifty of the young officers were there. The next morning Liu Ting came to see me and asked me to go with him to talk to Chou En-lai. I went to see him (Chou)--at Chang Hsüeh-liang's home. He was alone, walking back and forth, excited.

"He said: 'I am so worried, I am so worried. If this incident is resolved by t'ou-hsiang 投降 (surrender) now, then all is lost.

Everything you have said is correct. Now I know the difficulties which faced
Li Li-san 李立三   and Ch'en Tu-hsiu 陳獨秀 .'

"I said: 'You must do your best to change the situation.'"

Miao wanted Chou to persuade the Tung-pei generals to maintain the
alliance, and not to negotiate separately with Nanking, which doubtless
they were already doing. Chou must have feared that Colonel Sun's band
would kill the older generals and then perhaps internecine war would
destroy everybody, while only Chiang would benefit. He may have had in
mind the fateful decision made earlier by the Communists in Kiangsi, when
they failed to unite with the Nineteenth Route Army against Chiang Kai-
shek, in 1932-33, which cost them very heavily.

"Chou went to see Wang, Ho and Yü, but he did not succeed in convincing
them. Next morning Colonel Sun sent a car for me again to attend a meeting.
They asked me to agree to the assassination of Generals Wang and Ho. I
answered, 'Before taking this action let me consult with Chou.' Ying said,
'Don't talk to Chou. If you do, he will tell Wang, and Wang will kill us
first.' I asked if they would let me talk directly to Wang once more. They
said they would kill me if I did."

Miao did not agree to the young officers' plan but he did not oppose or
expose it.

"Ying then went to Tung-pei headquarters to direct the 'incident' and
I went to see Chou. After half an hour Liu Ting rushed in and told Chou
that Wang I-che had been killed, while Ho Chu-kuo's headquarters had been
surrounded. Chou said, 'This means there's only one way out.' He asked
us to arrest Chang Mu-t'ao 張慕陶   (Nanking's delegate?). I told
Colonel Sun to arrest him, which he did.

"Chou declared that it was war now, and he moved from Chang's home to
the lower floor (of another building). The Red Army was already alerted for
hostilities. When Chou returned from San Yuan he had shown me telegrams which
he himself had sent to various Red Army units ordering them to prepare for war.
'This is the first time I ever showed Red Army orders to any non-Communist
since I became a Red,' he told me. So I knew the Red Army now was ready to
fight.

"After Wang I-che was killed a meeting was called between Yang Hu-ch'eng,
Yü Hsüeh-chung and Chou En-lai. It was decided to order the Red Army to remain
in Weinan (south of the Wei River), but before the order was sent the
telephone line was cut. Liu To-ch'üan 劉多荃 (105th Tung-pei division)

sent a report saying he was retreating, being pursued. (He was a Tung-pei commander who had been sympathetic with the 'peace plan,' but also pro-Chou En-lai. He was now being pursued by forces of General Yang Hu-ch'eng, acting in collusion with the young officers.) When Chou heard Liu was retreating he again changed his mind. He now again advocated the peace plan. 'Even if I jump into the Yellow River I can never wipe it out. Everyone will blame me for (General) Wang's death,' he said."

A meeting was called between Chou, Yang Hu-ch'eng, Ho Chu-kuo and Yü Hsüeh-chung, where it was realized by all that the assassination of Wang had made it impossible for the policy of the "anti-negotiationists" to be supported against Nanking without provoking war not only against Nanking but also within the Northwest coalition itself. Miao himself apparently recognized this. The troops of Liu To-ch'üan and Yü Hsüeh-chung were outside the city walls and were prepared to attack the city, held by pro-Miao and pro-Sun troops.

"I (Miao) said: 'The only way is for me to leave the city with Sun and Ying. We can save Sian's people and leave the way open for a peaceful settlement between our army leaders.'

"Chou didn't believe me. Sun (Ming-chiu) was always obedient to me. I got hold of Ying and we three left the city and went to Yun-yang, where we were met by General P'eng Teh-huai. They welcomed us heartily; at the same time they held a memorial meeting for General Wang I-che. After we had been there a week we saw in the Hung-hsing pao (Red Star Daily) a story describing us as Trotskyists and childish, or Left-infantilists. I took this paper to P'eng and asked, 'What's the meaning of it? We killed Wang I-che, who was opposed to you. Why did you say we are Trotskyists?'

"P'eng replied, 'My comrade, you are foolish. If a bad thing like this happens, even if it doesn't originate with Trotskyism we may consider it as objectively Trotskyism.'

"I denied it was a bad thing. I said it resulted from a revolutionary demand. I said, 'I can't understand your revolution. You call a thing Trotskyist whether it is or not?'

"P'eng said, 'Some people say you are a madman. Perhaps you really are. Don't you know you have to take a curve? You can't go directly at a thing.'

"I said, 'Anyway I act honestly.'

"From this time on, the Central Government began to move the Northeast Army to Anhui (as a result of a negotiated settlement made by surviving Tung-pei generals). In the first month of the new Kuomintang-Communist party truce the Central Government gave the Red Army $500,000. The second month it gave only $250,000. P'eng became worried. They would not let us leave; they moved us to Tsun-hua, about 300 li from Yun-yang. This was in P'eng Teh-huai's territory. Hsiao K'e was also there."

Sun Ming-chiu rejoined the Tung-pei Army, but Miao and Ying were kept in the Red areas for some weeks, for a time in Kansu, "where we were treated like prisoners," according to Miao. Later, on appeal to P'eng, they were brought to the Yellow River and given $700 for traveling expenses and released in Shansi. From there they reached Peking by air.

"In Peking I met my friend Li who had just returned from six months in Sinkiang, where he was Chang Hsüeh-liang's representative or liaison man with General Sheng Shih-ts'ai 盛世才 (then governor of Chinese Turkestan). He told me, 'If the Sian Incident had led to civil war, then General Sheng would certainly have backed Chang Hsüeh-liang. He thought the Comintern did not know the real conditions in China and did not settle the Sian Incident in the right way.'"

I asked Miao whether Chou had advocated the release of Chiang Kai-shek from the moment he arrived in Sian, or whether he had changed his policy after receiving new directives.

"When Chou first went to Sian," Miao answered, "he wanted to put Chiang on public trial. But Chou got a telegram from Moscow and changed his mind. Sun and Ying told me Chang Hsüeh-liang was very worried about the Red Army's change of attitude. Chang Hsüeh-liang then wanted to liquidate the incident when he discovered (1) that the Red Army's attitude was so weak, and (2) that Chiang Kai-shek himself opposed Chang Hsüeh-liang's going to Nanking, saying, 'This won't be good for you.'"

5. Po Ku on Sian

Following is a transcription of part of my notes of an interview with Po Ku, Chinese Communist Party Politburo member and former party secretary, at this time deputy chief, under Chou En-lai, of the Eighth Route Army mission at Hankow.

<u>July 24, 1938</u>. <u>About Sian</u>. Po Ku arrived at Sian on December 24, bring-
ing orders from Pao-an. These he conveyed to Chou En-lai. Chou that night
after 10:00 p.m. went to see Chiang for the first time. Before then Chiang
had refused to see him. He was persuaded to do so chiefly by Mme Chiang and
by Donald and Chang Hsüeh-liang. At the meeting Chiang's first words were,
"We must not have any more civil war." It was the chief demand of the Communists that he make such a promise. After that he merely made some super-
fluous remarks saying, "All the time we've been fighting I often thought of
you. I remembered even during war that you had worked well for me. I
hope we can work together again."

Chiang was released entirely on Chang Hsüeh-liang's initiative,
according to Po Ku. Po had orders to get further assurances from Chiang,
but Mme Chiang had great influence here on the sentimental Chang Hsüeh-liang.
She kept saying she hoped Chang would give them a Christmas present by
releasing them and there could then be forgiveness all around. Chang
Hsüeh-liang fell for this. Po Ku did not know Chang intended to free
Chiang at the time. He had been called out to a meeting with others--
Tung-pei men--to persuade them, in principle, of the wisdom of releasing
Chiang. Po still favored holding Chiang until he made an "open statement"
promising to change his policy. Chou sent for him to talk to Chang Hsüeh-liang
at 2:00 P.M., but the message was delayed and he did not arrive until 3:00
P.M., when he learned that Chang Hsüeh-liang had already left (with Chiang
and Mme).

Chang Hsüeh-liang and Mme both told Chiang he could not be released
without seeing Chou. After their first meeting Chou saw Chiang on Christmas
morning, when Chiang again said he wanted an end to civil war. (In answer
to another question Po on second thought guessed that Chou might have been
able to see Chiang before, but had been waiting for Po Ku's arrival from
Pao-an with Red Army terms.) The Communists made Chiang no promises whatever
prior to his release, according to Po.

Po Ku claims that he himself was in favor of holding Chiang till January
first. He thought there was little danger of war (with the Nanking generals).
There was a risk, he thought, that if war did begin the Japanese might have
intervened to back Sung Che-yüan 宋哲元 (Hopei warlord) and Han Fu-ch'ü
韓復渠 (Shansi) to lead a five-province autonomous government supported by
the Japanese.

Po Ku thinks the situation today might be much better if (1) Chiang had been held a few days longer, and (2) Chang Hsüeh-liang had not gone to Nanking. Chou did everything he could to persuade Chang not to go. It was his own decision and he left without bidding Chou and Po Ku goodby, although they were staying in his house. When Chou learned of it he immediately got into a car and rushed to the airfield, arriving just in time to see the plane leaving. The field at the time was crowded with people, expecting to see Fu Tso-yi 傅作義 arrive. Nobody realized Chang, Chiang, Mme and Donald were leaving. Chang Hsüeh-liang acted this way because of his hero complex (says Po). Shortly after arriving in Nanking he regretted it; so said a letter he wrote to Sian.

Chang justified himself fully before the farcical mock trial (court martial), saying that he had released Chiang only to save the country from war, but as for the rest of the generals he said, "As soon as I get out of this I'll start a revolution and all of you will be through." He has not repented since his arrest. Chiang still fears him. All around Chiang are generals who remind him of the disgrace whenever the subject of Chang's release comes up. Po says the Communists have repeatedly requested it, only to be told, "The time is not yet."

Why has no greater agitation for it been led by the Communists? "Chang Hsüeh-liang's release is identified now with the interests of the revolution itself. Since the Communists for the sake of the United Front have given up so much in the way of advanced slogans of the revolution, we cannot agitate for a single man to the point of jeopardizing the nation's whole unity. But changes are occurring in the country, and when power changes Chang Hsüeh-liang will again have a role and the Communists will get him released."

Po Ku says the alleged speech of admonition delivered by Chiang (as reported in his book, Sian: A Coup d'Etat) was entirely fictitious. It was never made. It was all composed after he returned to Nanking, to present to the outside world to save face. This is known to everyone in Sian. Distribution of his speech has now been stopped. The real story of Sian may be known only when Chang Hsüeh-liang and Chou En-lai add their versions.

Note: Red Star Over China was in print before the foregoing facts came into my possession, and it was some years before I understood their full significance. An opportunity arose to modify the accepted interpretation of the Sian Incident in 1944, when the Modern Library included Red Star Over China in its uniform editions. I considered the problem of documenting the new facts for that purpose, but I could not have named several of my most important informants. I realized also that extensive changes would be necessary to bring all the rest of the book up to date, so much so that it would emerge as an almost different work. I concluded that a new book rather than a rewriting of the old one would be a better answer.

In my preface to the Modern Library edition of Red Star Over China I told of my decision to let the original text stand as a product of the time of the events described rather than take advantage of hindsight or afterknowledge.

I first referred to the Moscow telegram in print in a Saturday Evening Post article entitled "Will China become a Russian satellite?" dated April 9, 1949. As far as I know, that was the first published reference to it made anywhere.

II. PO KU 博古 (CH'IN PANG-HSIEN 秦邦憲)

1. Personal History

Po Ku was one of the more personable and interesting of the Communist leaders I met, and the youngest member of the Politburo. He was above average height and very thin and wiry--literally so, for he seemed almost strung on wires, his bodily movements being jerky and ill-coordinated. He had a high, nervous laugh, prominent teeth, and exophthalmic eyes which, especially behind his thick-lensed glasses, seemed to be popping out of his head. Sir Archibald Clark-Kerr used to call him "The Gollywog." He liked to play tennis -- and poker. He wore his hair cut short with a stiff brush on top. His mind was very quick and as subtle as, and perhaps more supple than, Chou En-lai's.

Po Ku told me his story in Pao-an, Shensi, in July 1936. Speaking in English he said:

"My father was a hsien-chang in Ningpo-hsien, Chekiang, until his death. I was then ten. My mother is still living in Wusih, Kiangsu, our native place. I attended primary school in Wusih and graduated from the Soochow Second Provincial Technical School, where I studied between 1921 and 1925.

"In 1925 I was elected president of the Student Union of Soochow. I joined the Kuomintang and Socialist Youth. Because of my political activity I fell behind in my studies and failed to get the proper credits to graduate. The director of the school was anxious to see the last of me, however, and gave me a diploma anyway. Thus I was able to enter Shanghai University-- which was sponsored by the Kuomintang and closed down a short time after the (Nationalist) revolution. I entered there in the fall of 1925. In October I joined the Communist party and soon afterward I left the university to spend my full time in political work.

"At this time I met Ch'ü Ch'iu-pai 瞿秋白 , who was a professor of social science at Shanghai University. Ch'ü was killed in 1935 after his capture in Tingchow, Fukien. In Shanghai I also met Ch'en Tu-hsiu. I participated in the Second Shanghai Uprising and left there soon afterward for Moscow, where I arrived in November 1926. I studied there at Sun Yat-sen University until May 1930. Then (on return) I worked in the All-China Trade-Union Federation, in Shanghai. I soon joined the opposition to Li Li-san, led by Wang Ming."

At that time, as Po said elsewhere, only four members of the Central Committee opposed Li Li-san: Wang Ming, Wang Chia-hsiang 王稼祥 , Po Ku and Ho Chih-shu [Ho Meng-hsiung 何夢雄 ?]. Po Ku said that Wang Ming was the most effective leader of the party—meaning the urban Central Committee—after the overthrow of Li, and even after Hsiang Fang-wu [Hsiang Chung-fa 向忠發] became secretary.

Concerning Li Li-san, Po said:

"His mistake was putschism. He favored armed uprisings, attempts to seize factories through armed struggle of the workers, collectivization in the soviet districts, capture of the big cities by armed attack. Li Li-san controlled the party line from 1929 to the end of 1930. He attempted an armed uprising in Pootung, the Shanghai industrial area, and in Nanking and Wuhan, by means of 'forced strikes.' The effect was to demoralize the workers, weaken the Red Army, and intensify the White terror. Basically he denied the practicability of rural soviets; he considered that the Red Army should mobilize for the storming of cities. Li ordered the attack on Changsha, which was at first successful. The second attempt was disastrous. Although it created a great sensation, the whole Changsha episode is now considered a serious mistake. Li had planned, after the first attack on Changsha, to go on from there to take Wuhan, and then the whole upper Yangtze Valley. He wanted Outer Mongolian forces to join in and support uprisings and civil war in Manchuria and North China. He was against the redistribution of land. He acted against the Comintern line. His mistake was that he insisted that China was, in 1930, in an 'imminently revolutionary situation,' and 'the center of the world revolution,' thus denying the Soviet Union as that center."

Po Ku emphasized Wang Ming's role in post-Li leadership, but did not mention Chou En-lai as an anti-Li Li-sanite. He said:

"Li had been in charge of Shanghai trade union organization; after he left I took a leading part in union organization. I edited Shang-hai kung-jen (Shanghai Worker) in close association with Hu Yeh-p'ing 胡也頻 , and contributed to the Red Flag Daily News, the Central Committee organ. With the removal of Li Li-san from the Central Committee, the leadership nominally passed to Hsiang Chung-fa, but in practice other leaders such as Wang Ming became prominent.

"After 1931 I took charge of the Communist Youth organization--and during the Manchurian Incident I participated in party discussions on policy. The Central Committee at its first meeting on the subject adopted the slogan, 'Arm the masses for revolutionary warfare against Japanese imperialism,' so that the line has not wavered until today. At that time we did not place so much emphasis on winning over the army to revolutionary resistance to Japan.

"In Shanghai I led the organization of volunteer workers to join the Nineteenth Route Army, as part of our '<u>Shang-hai chan-cheng chih-i ch'ü-te sheng-li</u>' Movement (Win Victory in Shanghai War--?). Commander Weng Chao-yuan 翁照垣 was then a strong Nationalist and two to three hundred Communists joined his army to attempt to win over troops for the revolutionary war of resistance. Many were killed. I organized strikes in various Shanghai cotton mills affecting forty thousand workers, men and women, but these were broken up by Japanese capitalists who made some compensation to the workers, and by the success of the yellow unions in getting control and arbitrating.

"In the autumn of 1932 the first proclamation of the Red Army appeared, offering the nation a program for united resistance against Japan, freedom of organization, cessation of civil war, and arming of the masses. This was the forerunner of our present program. The publication of this proclamation was the last act of the Central Committee in Shanghai when I left for Kiangsi."

Po Ku was in 1936 "minister for foreign affairs" and "chairman" of the Northwest government. He was married to Liu Ch'ün-hsien 劉羣仙, who made the Long March with Po and was a leading member of the women's department of the party. She was a native of Wusih, like Po, and a former cotton-mill worker. They met while students in Moscow--she was just his age--and married there. He spoke Russian and appeared to be the interpreter for Li Teh (German adviser) in all his conversations with Mao Tse-tung. He spoke quite intelligible English and read it with ease. He seemed on better terms with Li Teh than any other top leader. Li Teh spoke English, but practically no Chinese. I got the impression that Po Ku was not very popular with the army; he had no direct role in military affairs. When Po Ku was secretary of the party (1934) in Kiangsi, Li Teh was still a potent political as well as military figure. I assume that Moscow directives and communiqués were funneled through Li Teh and Po Ku in the first instance. They had already worked together for some time before Li Teh entered Kiangsi. Li Teh was in China at least as early as 1933, and possibly earlier.

The arrest of Noulens in Shanghai in 1930 may have contributed importantly to the discrediting of the Comintern line--now so-called Li Li-san line--of the time. It also marked closer cooperation between the foreign police and the Kuomintang, and increasing effectiveness of the White terror. Meanwhile, real power of decision and important problems of command obviously were shifting from the metropolis to the rural soviets. Perhaps Li Teh's departure for the interior finalized the subordination of the urban Central Committee to the party-military machine Mao Tse-tung had built up in the interior and which the "immigrants" and "returned students" attempted, but failed, to seize from his grasp.

My impression, without having made any recent or systematic study of material available which may bear on this question, is that Li Teh was the last or trump card used by Wang Ming--working on the Moscow end--and Po Ku in that struggle. With the discrediting of Li Teh and Po Ku after the mistake of rejecting an alliance with the Nineteenth Route Army, and the erroneous strategy and tactics blamed for the Reds' defeat in 1934, Mao's prestige was solidified in the army as well as in the party.

It is interesting that Mao handled Po Ku generously despite the latter's struggle against him, widely known throughout the party. Long after Mao's position became secure Po Ku was given positions of trust in the Central Committee. Li Teh also continued to be treated with respect and Mao frequently went through the motions of consulting him. Stalin would probably have wiped out both men.

Po Ku was still a member of the Politburo when he was killed in an airplane crash on April 8, 1946.

2. Interviews at Pao-an, October 1936

Po Ku said that the first soviet was organized by P'eng Pai 彭湃 at Hailufeng, 1927, but that the date December 11, 1927 is usually regarded as the beginning of the communist revolution. That was the uprising to form the Canton Commune. In 1930 the first Soviet government was set up in Kiangsi. Its first chairman was Ch'en Cheng-jen 陳正人 . Tseng Shan 曾山 was second chairman, elected in 1931. The first All-China Soviet Congress was held on December 11, 1931, the fourth anniversary of the Canton Commune.

The First Soviet Congress was attended by four to five hundred delegates, including representatives from Fang Chih-min's 方志敏 soviet (Tenth Army), K'ung Ho-ch'ung's 孔荷寵 (now a renegade) Sixteenth Army, Hsiao K'e's 蕭克 Eighth Army (Hunan-Kiangsi border district), P'eng Pai's region of Kwangtung, Hainan (a delegate named Chung Yeh), and Ho Lung's Second Army. The First Army Corps (Hupeh-Hunan-Anhui) was not represented. Other delegates came from Shanghai, Hongkong, Canton and Korea. Altogether they claimed to represent eight to ten million people, including peasant and labor unions. It was at that congress that Chu Teh was elected commander-in-chief. He remains so to this date.

Mao Tse-tung was elected first political commissar of the Red Army in 1932, at the same congress. Chou En-lai replaced him the next year and served till 1935. Mao was chairman of the Soviet Government.

I asked Po Ku whether the social and political conservatism of the peasantry and their religious superstitions and ethics did not make it a formidable task to win any genuine adherents to communist philosophy in this area.

All have their influence (he said). Perhaps the greatest obstacle is the traditional conservatism. Religious opposition plays no great role; it is not nearly so serious an obstacle to acceptance of revolution as in India or Russia, for example. Cultural and political backwardness of the masses delays the ready acceptance of new ideas and makes the peasant's attitude toward the Red Army, that of women in particular, at first one of suspicion and later of mere idle curiosity. It is hard to get anyone to come to meetings at first; then a few men come and then they persuade the women to come. They reach a stage after about six months (of occupation) where men and women actually hold hot debates.

Once land redistribution has actually occurred they begin to believe we are serious (he continued). Before that they believe nothing. About six months is necessary to convert skeptical peasants into active responsible workers. At early meetings the only questions raised are about taxes. Next comes the question of food. Then we begin to talk about the biggest landowner and agitate for confiscation. One or two landlords are mentioned and then more and more; peasants realize the Reds mean business.

Usually the first meeting is attended by only a few; the rest are cautious. In Szechwan it was different; many hundreds poured out at once; some women were so poor they hadn't even rags to cover them and came anyway, naked. As a rule we use dramas to call people together for the first meetings; the dramas are political in content and explain the Red Army.

3. Interviews at Hankow, July 23-24, 1938

a. Criticism of Red Star

Red Star Over China had been attacked in the Communist party press in
the United States and had been banned from its bookshops. It was
criticized for my remarks concerning the role of the Comintern in
China under Stalin's leadership and later. It was said that I had
imposed Trotskyist views on Mao Tse-tung's comments and that I was
hostile to the Communist Party of the Soviet Union.

Heinz Shippe, apparently an ex-Communist of German orgin, had been
living in Shanghai and writing reports and essays under the name
"Asiaticus." He wrote one long communication which was published
in Pacific Affairs,* in which he attempted to prove that I had
misrepresented the position of the Chinese Communist Party both with
regard to the theory and the practice of its policy during the
period of the United Front. He also, independent of the criticism
of the Communist Party of the United States, contended that I had
been under Trotskyist delusions. He held that the Chinese Communist
Party actually had given up the struggle for "leadership" of the
revolution under the slogans and policies of the United Front. He
insisted that they had genuinely recognized the Kuomintang as the
leader of the revolution and that as the United Front was a
bourgeois concept, no question of Communist party leadership in it
could arise.

It was my view, as expressed in Red Star Over China and elsewhere, that
the Chinese Communist Party had not at all given up its claims to
leadership of the peasants and workers, the majority of the people;
that it considered the United Front merely the most favorable form in
which to continue the struggle for fulfillment of those claims; that
it had never for even a moment abandoned its major long-term objectives
of a complete socialist revolution led by and under the hegemony of
and dictatorship of the Communist party.

In these interviews with Po Ku I sought to get a clear statement of
the Chinese Communist Party position on these questions. Two days
before I saw Po Ku in Hankow I met "R. A." there. He had already had
an account of Mao Tse-tung's attitude toward Heinz Shippe for his
attack on Red Star Over China. He said that Shippe had had a
translation made of his first and second articles on this subject
and forwarded it to Yenan. He had then proceeded there in person,
arriving in the spring of 1938. Here are my notes of the report I
got from R. A. of his conversation on this subject with Wang Ping-nan:

R. A. told me of Heinz Shippe's reception in Yenan. He arrived; he
at once called on Mao; he immediately began to talk about me and Red Star
Over China. Mao listened to the end of his harangue, but said nothing.
Shippe then continued to talk in monologue; Mao still said nothing.

*Jan. 1938.

Dismayed by Mao's silence, he finally left. He was assigned to a cave and food was sent to him, but nobody went to see him. He finally became very agitated and asked to know what was the matter. He demanded (another) interview with Mao, which was finally granted.

On his arrival at Mao's headquarters Shippe said that he had come to discuss the political situation, but Mao cut him short at once and spoke to him about as follows:

"Now, about Snow's book. It was a serious mistake for you to attack it. Snow came here to investigate our situation when nobody else would, and helped us by presenting the facts. You did not come. Even if he later on did something which we detest, we will always remember that he did a great service for China. He was the first person to pave the way for establishing friendly relations necessary for a united front, and we will not forget that. For you to attack him now without reason is a counter-revolutionary act. If you repeat this offense we will order all our people to break relations with you and you cannot have any more connections with us."

This is what Wang Ping-nan told R. A.

Agnes Smedley told me Heinz Shippe told her after he came back from Yenan that Mao had given him a terrible lecture. "He was really too severe with me. He was really too cruel," Heinz kept repeating. Mao told Shippe that he already had a bad record as a counter-revolutionary and "rightist" and could not get himself reinstated by attacking the United Front on "rightist" grounds. He told him he must be a better revolutionary than this if he wished to be "reinstated."

Heinz Shippe at that time evidently aspired to return to the fold by way of the Chinese Communist Party. He was anxious to give people abroad, particularly the United States, the impression that he was an authority and spokesman for the Chinese Communist Party. After this period I lost track of him.

b. On Leadership

On the question of the "leadership role" (in the national resistance period) Po Ku said:

"The Kuomintang undoubtedly is leading the resistance as the holder of (major) political power. But Chiang is influenced by the Communist party. The Chinese Communist Party now says we possess the leadership from a tactical point of view.

"The question of leadership is the question of struggle for influence over the peasants, the petty-bourgeoisie and other middle forces of the democratic revolution. It cannot be separated from the mobilization of the people as a whole. Just now, during the time when the bourgeoisie is partici-pating in the revolution, the struggle for leadership is a real one and a democratic one. Only when the bourgeoisie turns counter-revolutionary is the question less important. Then the bourgeoisie becomes the enemy of the revolution. Victory of the revolution is no longer a question of the fight for leadership <u>after</u> the bourgeoisie becomes counter-revolutionary; it is then only a question of struggle under the <u>only</u> revolutionary leadership, or of surrender to the counter-revolution."

I then showed Po Ku Heinz Shippe's letter in <u>Pacific Affairs</u>, in which he denied that the Chinese Communist Party was in any way struggling for leadership. I pointed out Shippe's statement that "competition for leadership has never been a main question."

"This is nonsense," laughed Po Ku. "We must struggle for leadership everywhere and at all times. We do not deny that. A political party that does not lead has no reason for existence. Of course, right now we cannot talk about the struggle for proletarian leadership. (But) every Kuomintang leader knows that Stalin said, 'The struggle for proletarian leadership is the first stage in the struggle for proletarian dictatorship.' We don't want to frighten people by discussing such questions, but it is of course a fact that we compete for leadership and that we must do so. Only under the hegemony of the workers and peasants can the bourgeois-democratic revolution succeed."

In answer to a direct question concerning my chapters in <u>Red Star</u> on the Chinese Communist Party's past relations with the Comintern, Po Ku said: "You were a little too strong in your criticism. Everything you say is true, but the thing is: we don't wish to talk about these matters now."

c. On Party Make-up

I next asked him how they could contend that they had the leadership of the "workers" when in fact there were very few in the army or party and the Japanese occupation of the main industrial centers was cutting them off still more from the working class. "Without any true industrial proletariat in the interior to draw from, how will the Communist party continue to represent it as a class?"

Po Ku admitted that party work was extremely weak in Shanghai before and after the war. The organization had been practically destroyed. Liu Kuo-p'ing had been sent to organize Shanghai workers after Sian, but he was just getting started when war broke out. Actually, the occupation had made the work easier. Already the Chinese Communist Party had recruited two hundred workers for the New Fourth Army from Shanghai. More would soon be mobilized. Most of them were going directly into the army. Po Ku recognized the limitations of this method and the necessity for setting up some kind of production bases in the interior to attract workers. "This is one of the most important tasks before us. We must have trained workers in our districts."

On this point Po Ku conceded that a preponderance of students, petty-bourgeois in background, among new Communist party recruits made it difficult to maintain the labor point of view and interests. But Wuhan was better than Shanghai. Among new recruits in Hankow forty per cent or more were factory or other industrial workers. The party was now limiting the number of students admitted.

"There is a real danger of the party becoming dominated by the petty-bourgeois point of view if we take in too many intellectuals over a long period."

d. Schools

In answer to my questions Po Ku said that in July 1938 party membership was more than 200,000; that the greatest difficulties for party activity existed in Kiangsi, Kweichow and Shensi. Conditions were also bad in Kwangsi, but at least Red leaders there were not being arrested. There were about 120,000 regulars in the Eighth Route Army now; more than 100,000 partisans, variously and partly armed, now spread across Shensi, Shansi, Hopei, Chahar, Jehol and Shantung.

Training schools operated by the Reds by this time included the Anti-Japanese Military Academy in Yenan, with five to six thousand students. It offered a seven-and-a-half-month course. Lin Piao 林彪 was president. One section of students came from Red Army veterans. Another section (about five thousand) came from graduates of a Shen-pei kung-hsüeh, where students received an intensified four-month course in political and economic history. Ch'eng Fang-wu 成仿吾 and Fang Wen-ping [Feng Wen-pin 馮文彬 ?] were directors.

There were also a Preparatory School for Youth (four months), with one to two thousand students; Lu Hsün Art Academy (training of propagandists), with 200 students; Lu Hsün Normal School (six-month courses), with 200 students; Communist Party School under K'ang Sheng 康生 [pseudonym of Chao Jung 趙容] and Wang Ming, with about 500 students (ensconced in the Yenan Catholic Church); Mobile Training School (1,000 students who "learn and fight"); Chiao-tao Yin (Training Battalion found in every division headquarters, for advanced study in military and political techniques); and one military training school in Fu-p'ing (on Suiyuan border), headed by Nieh Jung-chen 聶榮臻 。

Students in all schools pay for their own food, or work for it. Mostly students get help from home. One student's father gave ten thousand dollars. A general assessment of one dollar per month is imposed on all officers.

4. Conversation at Chungking
(Diary excerpt dated October 9, 1939)

。。。。 Po Ku thought that Mao was attacking the British too strongly. He considers that Britain and the U.S.S.R. may yet get together against Germany; it is at least as possible as the other way around (England and Germany against Stalin). I told him the gist of my interviews* with Mao

---

*See China Weekly Review (Jan. 13 and 20, 1940).

on the international question, much of which were apparently elaborations on
what had already appeared in the Yenan press. Po Ku said they (the Chungking
Communist party office) had wired Mao to "leave America out" in his attacks
on "imperialist warmongers." Po Ku considers that China is now mainly dependent on the U.S.S.R. and the U.S.A. They could not afford to antagonize
the United States, especially since the U.S.S.R. policy also favors trying
to cooperate with America. At the recent (eighteenth?) Congress of the CPSU
it was stated that the United States was the only capitalist democracy which
is genuinely anti-fascist.

After hearing me quote from Mao's interview with me concerning
Chamberlain and Roosevelt, Po Ku shook his head and wondered if it was
necessary for me to publish it. As Communist representative on the spot,
who had to answer criticisms of non-Communist Chinese, as well as Westerners,
who felt that Stalin had betrayed the cause of progress and enlightenment
by his cynical deal to swallow one half of Poland while Hitler was inhaling
the other, Po Ku was (it seemed to me) more keenly aware of the "contradictions" in the Kremlin's turncoat policy than Mao, whose views went unchallenged
in Yenan.

III. LIN PIAO 林彪

1. Personal History

Lin Piao gave me the following facts in Pao-an, July 1936.

Lin was director of the Communist Military Academy in Pao-an, at the age of twenty-eight. He was on leave from the First Army Corps, of which he remained commander.

Born in Huang-an, Hupeh province, in 1908, Lin Piao was the son of middle-class parents. His father had owned a small handicraft factory which prospered briefly in the World War (I), but was bankrupted by exorbitant taxes imposed by local warlords. After his business failure his father got work as a purser on a Yangtze River Boat. In Pao-an Lin did not know whether his father was dead or alive. He had not seen him for many years.

Young Lin did not enter any school until he was nine; he then completed primary school work in five years and at thirteen entered a middle school, from which he graduated in 1924. Having determined to become a revolutionary soldier, he found his way to Canton and was admitted to the Whampoa Academy there soon after Bluecher took over. He graduated the next year and became a lieutenant.

Earlier, in Shanghai, Lin had joined the Young Socialist League, which helped him to enter Whampoa. In 1925 Chiang Kai-shek, president of Whampoa, ordered all students there to give up their dual membership in the Kuomintang and Communist party. They could join one or the other, but not both. The Young Socialist League had by then merged with the Young Communist League and Lin, who was also a member of the Kuomintang, had to choose. He left the Kuomintang and joined the Communist party.

During the Northern Expedition Lin Piao distinguished himself in Chang Fa-kuei's 張發奎 Fourth (Ironsides) Army and was promoted to captain in 1925, and to major in 1926. He was in the division led by Yeh T'ing 葉挺 , which, with one division of the Twentieth Army (Ho Lung's) and one division of the Eleventh Army, joined with Chu Teh's police garrison in the Nanchang Uprising that marked the beginning of the Red Army and its struggle for power against the Kuomintang under Chiang Kai-shek. The junta

at Nanchang called itself the Kuomintang Ke-ming Chün (Kuomintang Revolutionary Army). Their uprising having failed, Ho, Yeh and Chu fled southward,
some to Swatow, some to Canton, others to Hunan. Lin Piao's division went
to southern Hunan, where it arrived with about a thousand men. Here they
joined forces with Mao Tse-tung, formed the Workers and Peasants Red Army,
and for the first time adopted the Red Flag, in December 1927. From that time
Lin Piao remained a commander in the Red Army.

Lin participated in, and became noted for his tactical leadership
during the battles of Chingkangshan and Tsalin, where the first soviet was
formed in China, in March 1928. From Chingkangshan he later fought his way
to Ningtu (Kiangsi) and Juichin; he led troops along the Fukien and, still
later, the Szechwan borders. By 1929 he was commander of the Fourth Red
Army. He held that command under Chu Teh, as commander-in-chief, and Mao
Tse-tung, as political commissar, during the Red Army's first attack on
Changsha, in 1930. In January 1932 he was promoted to commander of the
First Red Army Corps, which contained the pick of their forces. It then
had about twenty thousand rifles. Later Lin commanded an "Eastern Army"
which included the Fifth, as well as the First, Army Corps. Nieh Jung-
chen was political commissar. The Fifth Corps had been under the command of
Chi Chen-t'ung 李振同 , "who joined the counter-revolution and was
imprisoned," according to Lin . . . .

Lin now became elusive as a personality as his own story merged
completely with the army and military actions in which he participated.
He had many successes in border warfare in towns on the Kiangsi-Fukien
and Kiangsi-Kwangtung borders. He remained a corps commander throughout
Chiang Kai-shek's second, third, fourth and fifth anti-Red extermination
campaigns. During all but the fifth campaign Lin was almost invariably
successful. The Reds captured many arms and continued to increase their
strength.

2. Comments on Kiangsi Warfare

Lin continued:
"The first battle of the Kuomintang's Fifth Offensive took place in
September 1933, on International Youth Day (second Sunday in September).

The First Corps was on the Ninth Front; the Third Corps went to Fukien and "established contact" with the Nineteenth Route Army. I commanded the First Corps. P'eng Teh-huai commanded the Third Corps.

"Our first battle was fought at Wuchang, Kiangsi. We disarmed a brigade of the Eightieth Division, under the command of Chiang Kai-shek's headquarters. In the same month there was a small battle at Tan-chang, in Lo-an-hsien, Kiangsi, and another at T'ai-fang, where one Kuomintang regiment was defeated and all its munitions and supplies were captured.

"After these initial battles of the Fifth Campaign the enemy adopted new tactics which we called 'fortism.' The enemy never leaves the direct protection of artillery sheltered by fortifications, and advances only a few hundred yards at a time. On this basis the enemy engaged us in another battle at Ta-shun-kuan, in Ni-huang-hsien, Kiangsi. Because of 'fortism' we could not carry out encirclement tactics, and the battle was indecisive.

"In the meantime Chiang Kai-shek was confronted by the Fukien rebellion of the Nineteenth Route Army. At that time we adopted a wrong policy. We are not afraid of self-criticism and may say this. Chiang was at that time on the defensive on both the west and north, against our forces and others, while he moved his army into the east against Fukien. At this time we should have attacked his rear, but instead we were ordered to attack the fort at Yun Fung and T'ien Tien, west of Ningtu, Kiangsi. The enemy's forts there were very strong and his troops were well paid and well equipped, being salt troops [i.e. anti-smuggling forces of the salt revenue administration] under T. V. Soong. We wasted a month there without any decision.

"It was not till early in 1934 that we began to move east for the purpose of helping the commanders of the Nineteenth Route Army, Chiang Kuang-nai 蔣光鼐 and Ts'ai T'ing-k'ai 蔡廷楷 ; but it was too late. Chiang Kai-shek moved too swiftly. He had mobilized eleven divisions, mostly withdrawn from Kiangsi, and moved them against Fukien. We failed to realize our objective: to unite with the Nineteenth Route Army to disarm Chiang Kai-shek's forces. Instead, Chiang defeated the rebels and turned to attack us.

"From then on Chiang Kai-shek relied on 'fortism.' He built so many forts--many thousands!--that they could virtually be connected by machine-gun fire. Each fort was defended by about sixteen men; important ones held as many as a company. Chiang's reason for 'fortism' was to deny us the use of maneuver for offensive tactics. He forced us to use defensive tactics against a 'defensive enemy,' and his defensive means were superior to ours.

"Only one battle in the fifth campaign could be considered a strategic success. At Wen-fang, near Tingchowfu, Fukien, the First Corps (first and second divisions) and the Twelfth Army (in all thirteen thousand men, under Lin Piao) met two enemy divisions on September 1, 1934. We disarmed one brigade during a night battle, which proved that 'fortism' could be defeated.

"The Kuomintang troops had already occupied the top of a large hill called Chu-tsung-ling, some thirty li long. North of it was another hill, Hu-mou-ling. Covered by forts, the enemy began advancing toward us. We divided our forces and went to meet them; after sunset we climbed toward the side of the hills. While the main forces were engaged on the hills, part of our forces attacked and entered the city, Tingchow, where we took a brigade by surprise. Not a horse escaped.

"This victory was due to our combining of defensive and offensive tactics, with a surprise attack on the enemy flank—our real objective.

"These tactics were against Li Teh's advice. After the fall of the town our forces ascended the Chu-tsung-ling and took important blockhouses. On the following day a second action occurred when we ambushed eight regiments of enemy troops attempting to reinforce the defeated troops. The result was a brigade commander captured, another brigade commander wounded, 160 officers captured, 2,300 prisoners, over 3,500 enemy casualties, and the capture of thousands of rifles, machine guns and other equipment.

"This victory was important because it proved that so-called 'fortism' could be defeated," Lin repeated.

Lin Piao gave me a list of the various captured materials. Then he reiterated that although it was a significant victory wrong tactics continued to be followed elsewhere. Despite their defeats "the unity and spirit of the Red Army was excellent."

Without any air force, the Reds defending forts (their own) were easy targets for enemy planes. "We lost 4,700 men by air bombing in the Second Division alone. Men in the forts became a fixed target. Many officers stayed at the forts after three or four wounds, without dressing. Many times they fought to the last man. It was a common thing for ordinary soldiers to take command of forts automatically after all officers were killed.

"Because of our mistakes in strategy and tactics we were unable to come to a decisive encounter with the Nanking troops. The methods of Comrade Li Teh resulted in scattering our forces and maintaining a continuous contact with the enemy, which was highly disadvantageous to us with our inferior equipment and resources. We were deprived of opportunities to maneuver and make the best use of our forces by massing them for quick attacks and quick dispersal."

Lin Piao read me the following excerpt from a book called War and Revolution, a chapter entitled "On the Short Attack," by himself:

"Our task is not to delay the advance of the enemy but to annihilate his living force. We ought to let the enemy advance according to their original plans. It is not necessary to resist them merely to delay them. (But this does not mean we should not send out partisan detachments to induce the enemy to advance.--Li Teh). Because the enemy, when resisted, will stop and build forts, and will thus decrease our opportunities to maneuver for major annihilating attacks. (But there are exceptions!--Li Teh)."

Lin's article appeared on July 5, 1934. He quoted Li Teh's parenthetical remarks scornfully, saying Li was opposed to the "short attack."* It was clear that he, at least, held the unfortunate German, Li Teh, mainly responsible for the Kiangsi defeat. As Lin was, in Pao-an, in a leading position of responsibility for tactical training of the army (head of the military academy), it seemed obvious that Mao and other Chinese commanders supported his view.**

Lin led a main column on the Long March to the Northwest. He was in the vanguard during most of the advance from Szechwan to Kansu and the new base around Pao-an, and he led the First Corps in the Shansi expedition. He also smashed several Tung-pei (Manchurian) divisions in the winter of 1935-36, when much valuable equipment was acquired.

---

* A term invented by Lin Piao to describe this kind of maneuvering warfare, in which he became a recognized expert.

** See Chou En-lai's remarks, p. 60; also Hsiao Ching-kuang, p. 32.

Associated with Chou En-lai from the earliest days at Canton, in 1924-25, a veteran of Nanchang, with Chu Teh, a veteran of the bitter winter with Mao Tse-tung atop Chingkangshan, 1927-28, a trusted commander of the victorious Communist armies in Manchuria and North China, 1948-49, and a top commander during the Korean war, Lin appears to be next in line after P'eng Teh-huai for the supreme army command. Though perhaps outranked on a seniority basis by men like Ho Lung, Hsiao K'e, Lo P'ing-hui 羅丙輝 , Nien Jung-chen, Yeh Chien-ying 葉劍英 , and others, his combat record over the entire period from Nanchang to date has scarcely been equalled.

IV. HSIAO CHING-KUANG 蕭勁光

1. Personal History

A tall, strongly built soldier, thirty-four years old, Hsiao is a
native of Hunan, where he received elementary and middle school education.
One of the earliest of Chinese students in Russia (1920-24), he returned to
China at the time of the Sun-Joffe agreement. He graduated from Whampoa
Academy and participated in the Northern Expedition. After the counter-
revolution he was sent to Russia, where he remained from 1927 to 1931.
On his return to China he went to the Kiangsi soviets and took command
of the Seventh Army Corps, which he led until the Long March. During the
Shansi Expedition (1935) he helped recruit and organize the Twenty-ninth
Independent Army, made up of some veteran cadres and 8,000 men enlisted
in Shansi and brought back across the Yellow River. At the time of my
interview with him, Hsiao was commander of the Twenty-ninth Army.

Hsiao's wife, also a returned student from Russia, was arrested in
Shanghai four years before this, during her work in the "anti-Japanese
movement" there following the Japanese invasion and the period of the
"great arrests." Hsiao has one son studying in Moscow, another in
Shanghai.

In Inside Red China Nym Wales reported Hsiao's wife had been released
from prison.

2. Interview

August 12, 1936. . . . Hsiao thinks it necessary first to enlarge the
United Front before anything like a serious attack can be made directly on
Japanese forces in China. If there is war it will be positional warfare in
its early stages, and the Red Army is weak there. It must get much greater
technical experience and equipment. Under present conditions Red strength is
most effective in guerrilla warfare and partisan tactics.

He cited the example of the Kiangsi disaster when an attempt was made
to fight a war of positions in the Fifth Campaign. This was due largely
to Li Teh's advice. When Li Teh first arrived he was very confident and

very authoritative. He pounded his fist on the table. He told Mao and the others that they knew nothing about military matters; they should heed him. How was he able to do that? He had, of course, the "prestige of the world communist supporters behind him."

Hsiao believes Russia will and must help China in war against Japan, and will certainly defend the revolution against Japanese imperialism.

V. THE LAND REVOLUTION

1. Wang Kuan-lan 王 觀 瀾

Wang Kuan-lan, chairman (or minister) of the Land Commission of the
Northwest Branch of the Central Soviet Government, 1936, was born in Ling-
hai-hsien, Chekiang in 1908. He came from a poor family, his father was
a wood carver, and he was an only child. Wang attended provincial normal
school at Ling-hai for two years. In 1926 he joined the Communist Youth.
The following year he joined the party and was sent to the U.S.S.R.
There he studied three years at the Eastern Toilers University--formerly
Sun Yat-sen University--where he learned to speak and read Russian.

At the end of 1930 Wang returned to China and went to the Kiangsi
Soviet. He was chosen chairman of the Agitation-Propaganda Bureau of
the Central Committee. He also acted as chairman of the Hsing-kuo-hsien
party committee and head of the political department of the Red Guards.
In 1932 he became editor of the Central Soviet Government's official
paper, Hung-se Chung-hua (Red China). He became vice-chairman of the
Land Commission in 1933, and in 1934 joined the political department of
the Central Government. He made the Long March and on arrival in Shensi
was appointed (by the Central Committee) to his present post.

In Moscow Wang studied: history of communism, problems of Leninism,
problems of the Chinese revolution, world political history, economic
geography.

2. Communist Land Policy and Practice

An interview with Wang Kuan-lan, July 30, 1936.

Wang Kuan-lan said:

"There are two revolutions in China; one is anti-imperialist,
-the other is about the land question. Land is considered a fundamental

issue of the revolution, a problem which must be solved.

"According to laws adopted by the First All-China Soviet Congress, the landlords and gentry must be deprived of their property. Land of the rich absentee owners is distributed to farmers according to their labor capacities and needs. There is no interference with land-owning tillers. Poor peasants and farm workers are given land such as they can till profitably. The property of religious organizations is also confiscated in accordance with the law.

"Basically, there are two methods of land distribution: (1) distribution in accordance with the labor power of the population; that is, the contribution of the individual's labor power to value produced; and (2) according to the total population; that is, (a 'fair') division to each family. Adjustments are constantly made between these two methods so as to achieve fairness without impairing production. The people have the right to decide about such matters in a mass vote. The process is called fen-p'ei (divide) by the Communists--not hsin san-pu ('redistribute').

"High interest rates and high taxes and levies are abolished. Debts are liquidated, thus lifting crushing burdens from the poor and middle peasants. Crop-sharing ends, of course."*

Concentration of Land Ownership

Following are Wang's estimates of comparative concentration of land ownership in Kiangsi and Shensi, based on statistics compiled by workers in the Land Commission.

---

*See p. 37.

	Kiangsi	Shensi
Landlords (owner does not labor; rents out land; has large holdings; hires labor; lends money; may or may not be absentee, but personally does not work on land)		
Percentage of population	3-4	Less than 1
Percentage of land owned	20-30	See below
Rich farmers (proprietors who own land, hire labor and lend money, but also do some tilling themselves)		
Percentage of population	5-6	3-4
Percentage of land owned	20	See below
Middle farmers (farmers who own land; they till and sometimes hire labor and lend a little money, but usually are in debt to usurers)		
Percentage of population	20-30	20-30
Percentage of land owned	30	See below
Poor peasants (tenant farmers who own little or no land and sometimes hire out as labor; always in debt to usurers)		
Percentage of population	30-50	40-50
Percentage of land owned	20	See below
Farm workers (bankrupt farmers or idle peasants or workers who hire themselves out for farm work)		
Percentage of population	8-9	7-8
Percentage of land owned	Nil	Nil
Merchants, clerks, traders, peddlers (includes also priests, teachers, rural beggars and unemployed, militia, etc.)		
Percentage of population	10-19	5-10
Percentage of land owned	0-10	Very little
TOTALS:		
Percentage of population	76-109	86-103
Percentage of land owned	90-110	See below

   <u>Comment on tables</u>. Wang was speaking of the peasant or rural farming population, and "merchants, clerks," etc. referred only to village inhabitants, not cities. No workers or bourgeoisie, per se, are included. He said estimates generally applied to most provinces south of the Yangtze in which the Reds operated, but since overall statistics had never been gathered he could only give a range of averages within his knowledge. He was sure that his estimates for Kiangsi, which showed eight to ten per cent of the population owning from forty to fifty per cent of the land, applied pretty generally in the more densely populated and rich farming areas.

   Wang continued: "The above figures are based only on hsien in the north of Shensi, and even here statistics are far from complete. Conditions vary exceedingly. Landlords around Mi-te and Sui-te, for example, collect 2,000 to 3,000 <u>tan</u> (3,000 piculs or about 600 tons) of millet in rent income annually, from 2,000 to 3,000 <u>shang</u> of land (1 <u>shang</u> = 3-5 <u>mou</u>), or (say) 6,000 to 12,000 <u>mou</u>. In Sui-te there are large landholders on this scale--at least four or five families. Farther south the situation is quite different; in some places there is more land than available tillers can till.

   "With the change in communist policy in line with the aims of the United Front, the land policy has also changed. At present estates are still expropriated, but the landlords are allowed to retain for their own use land sufficient to provide them an average income. Secondly, the land of rich peasants is no longer divided. Owners of farm enterprises are not expropriated as long as they remain on the land as managers or producers. In certain cases, if the peasants vote to confiscate a rich peasant's land, it will be divided. The Communists no longer emphasize this, however, and even if the peasants insist on it, the rich peasant family must still be allowed a portion to cultivate for its own needs.

   "In other words, the government will not encourage confiscation of any land except large estates, in this period. We are experimenting to see whether the poor peasants' support can be won without large-scale redistribution. The land owned by petty bourgeoisie (small merchants, shop owners, technical workers, teachers, etc.) is not confiscated. Land owned by anti-Japanese officers and officials is not being confiscated. Liquidation of

debt is no longer general, but in accordance with revised laws there is
reduction of interest to ten per cent, except in the case of major usurers,
where debts are wiped out completely (i.e., debts between poor peasants and
merchants or small money lenders are honored but controlled). Land rentals
are no longer completely abolished, but rents are limited to twenty-five
per cent of the crop. Usury is not prohibited, but as Soviet law makes it
possible for peasants to borrow and buy goods or grain on non-interest-
bearing loans, with repayment to be made after the harvest, usury in
effect disappears."

Agricultural Stations

"In Kiangsi there were fifty to sixty students in an agricultural
school which graduated a new class every three months. The school experimented
with different crops, seeds, soils, fertilizers, and so on. They studied
crop diseases and pests and made experiments with remedies. Graduates were
sent to different hsien to help the farmers and to set up agricultural stations. Courses were rudimentary but practical and brought in techniques
of great interest and help to farmers. In Shensi Reds haven't yet set up
stations but are just beginning."

Collective Work

"The Society for Mutual Labor Help (Lao-tung chu-shih) under the Land
Commission (Ministry of Land) conducts propaganda among farmers urging them
to work together--in planting, tilling and marketing. Means are adopted to
promote greater production.

"One hsien in Kiangsi had 'labor mutuals' with 17,000 members. In
Shensi there are now altogether only about 20,000. Because of lack of
tools, animals and other necessities, the idea of collective help is very
readily accepted here and will spread rapidly. There is a bureau here
called 'bureau for adjusting corn and food supplies.'"

Cooperatives

"The government is encouraging the formation of cooperatives, with membership fees based on the amount and kind of land owned. Peasants who join are allowed to use the tools and the animals of the cooperative. In Kiangsi the government and the peasant cooperatives were separate; here they are combined. Following the enlargement of the Red Army in Shensi, there is a lack of labor in some villages, and productive cooperatives help meet the need. In Kiangsi and Fukien there were committees to train women to replace men in farm work and now they are being organized here also--Fu-nü hsüeh-hsi sheng-ch'an wei-yuan-hui."

Cultivation of Idle Land

"In Kiangsi the state took over wasteland and newly deserted land or lands owned by absentees. Such lands accounted for fifteen per cent of the total production in Kiangsi. In Hsing-kuo-hsien* the crop increase amounted to twenty per cent or more.

"As a result of the reclamation of such lands and their division among the peasants and Red Army families in Kiangsi, in one six-month period an additional 220,000 tan, or 660,000 mou, were brought into cultivation. As for North Shensi, from February to May of this year we brought into production about 1,700 shang (3-5 mou to a shang) of new lands reclaimed from wasteland or idle land. (That is, outside of the land re-division program.) Even though many young men joined the army, the crop increase continued.

---

*The Reds' so-called "model hsien."

<u>Table of Organization of the People's Land Committees</u>

Consists of four bureaus under a
planning committee, led by the minister
or commissioner of land. They are: (1) bureau
of expropriation and division of land; (2) bureau of
land reconstruction; (3) bureau of irrigation and for-
estry; (4) bureau of inspection, registration and statistics.

<u>Provincial Land Board</u>

Contains a planning committee and four
sub-bureaus corresponding to the above.

<u>Hsien Land Board</u>

Contains a planning committee and
sub-bureaus corresponding to the above.

<u>Ch'ü Land Board</u>

Consists of same committee and bureaus.

<u>Hsiang Land Board</u>

Contains a land committee which carries out
functions of all the bureaus mentioned above.

"The People"

<u>Elections</u>

"At present under emergency conditions the officials of the State
Land Committee are appointed, but locally they are elected, and it is the
aim to have all elected. In Kiangsi a popular election was held to elect
All-Soviet representatives to the Congress.

"The election laws which govern formation of the state and local governments were set forth in the Soviet Constitution adopted by the Soviet Congress
in Kiangsi. At present it is in abeyance.

"In practice here the local land committees are chosen by the peoples' revolutionary committees, after a place is occupied. The local committee decides what land confiscations to make and calls upon the various higher bureaus to carry out their decisions. One who is being expropriated can appeal to the people's land committees right to the central committee for a hearing. Or he can appeal to the peasants and workers unions. If the committee concerned does not observe the opinion of the Inspection Bureau, then the case is taken to the ministry or state commission.

"All this is provisional, to be regulated when conditions are stabilized and popular elections can be held.

"Now, of course, it is a dictatorship of the revolution under party hegemony."

VI. STATE SECURITY

1. Chou Hsing 周興

Chou was born in Yuan-feng, Kiangsi, in 1908. His parents were handicraft workers. He studied three years in primary school and three years in higher primary. Then he became a shop apprentice. In 1925 a student talked to him and interested him in the revolution; he joined the Communist Youth. During the Great Revolution he joined the party and was ordered to work in the Peasant Union. Later he was assigned to study in Chu Teh's military police academy in Nanchang, but he became ill and stayed with Fang Chih-min 方志敏 in the Peasant Union. Fang joined Mao Tse-tung, and Chou and he participated in the Tung-ku peasant uprising. From then until 1930 he led a peasant partisan detachment. In 1930 he had worked with the Pao-wei Chü (police) of the partisans, and subsequently he specialized in the organization of partisan nuclei.

From the thirties until he made the Long March to the Northwest he was active in the suppression of counter-revolutionaries.

Chou is unmarried now (October 1936), though he "had a wife for a few days before he left home" (Kiangsi).

2. State Security Problems and Justice

An interview with Chou Hsing, chief of the National Political Defense Bureau (Kuo-chia Cheng-chih Pao-wei Chü), October 9, 1936.

I asked Chou Hsing the following questions:

1. What are the offenses for which people are subject to arrest and punishment by the Gaypayoo? In what cases is the death sentence applied?

2. Does the Gaypayoo arrest, try and punish political offenders, or turn them over to people's courts? When is "on-the-spot justice" administered?

3. What police forces do you have at your command?

4. What is the difference between present and past (Kiangsi) security policy?

5. Is there a "regular" police system in Shensi in addition to yours?

6. How does the Soviet government treatment of political prisoners differ from that of the Kuomintang?

Chou Hsing said:

"The Kuo-chia Cheng-chih Pao-wei Chü, or National Political Defense Bureau, does not use the term 'Gaypayoo,' which is inexact as applied by outsiders. Its duty is to safeguard the revolution wherever it achieves victory. Counter-revolutionaries do not cease their activities after the Red Army arrives. In order to oppose them, the Pao-wei Chü relies upon the help of the masses and upon educational methods to change the ideas of counter-revolutionists, especially those who are unconsciously counter-revolutionary.

"The Pao-wei Chü is not so dreadful. Its policy is simply to protect the soviet power, and now it is to expand the United Front.

"In Kiangsi the definition of a counter-revolutionary was more rigid than it is now during the United Front period. Then, nobody was talking to us about cooperation against the imperialists; now, it is different. In Kiangsi anybody who did not sympathize with us was regarded as counter-revolutionary. His property was confiscated, and if he was anti-Soviet he was deprived of rights, even though he might take no positive action against us.

"In Kiangsi our policies were formed solely in the interest of the main elements of the population who actively supported the revolution. The funda-mental difference now is that we recognize a new category of people, who are anti-Japanese on the one hand, but may not be in sympathy with the Communists on the other hand. Such people are not subject to arrest, punishment or discrimination, as long as they don't attempt, by violence, to overthrow the soviet power. We try to educate such people and struggle with them ideolog-ically, but not by force or coercion. Secondly, we don't dispossess such people by the agrarian revolution, but we allow them their land. Thirdly, we adopt a moderate policy toward them politically.

"In other words, the Pao-wei Chü now not only protects the victories of the revolution but also protects the basis of the United Front."

Answers to questions:

1. "Anyone who attempts to organize an [anti-communist] meeting, upris-ing, or wholesale desertion is subject to arrest by the Pao-wei Tui. Anyone

attempting or planning an assassination will be arrested. Anyone found doing espionage work will be arrested. People who organize or try to organize mass anti-social or counter-revolutionary work will be arrested. People who spread rumors or lies about the Red Army will be subject to arrest and punishment in accordance with the offense.

"Nobody is arrested for merely expressing an opinion or saying something against the regime, but consistent exposition of anti-Soviet views is not allowed and is punishable.

"Punishment varies according to the seriousness of the offense and includes imprisonment, hard labor, deportation, 'education,' and so on. The death sentence is now very seldom applied, and only when the individual is very much hated by the masses.

"The majority of political prisoners are subjected to brief periods of detention and intensive political indoctrination. Where the nature of the offense clearly shows that the prisoner was consciously counter-revolutionary and actively instigating counter-revolutionary activity, it may be worse. Leaders of armed anti-communist organizations are sometimes shot, but their followers are treated moderately. The whole personal history of the individual prisoner is taken into consideration before any judgment is made."

2. "Local courts do exist in the hsiang, ch'ü, hsien and provincial centers. When a prisoner is tried in a local court the soviet government calls a mass meeting and elects two representatives to the local jury, while the soviet government appoints a judge. Every ch'ü has a justice department which appoints the judge for each trial; or the chairman of the justice department may preside. There is also a procurator appointed by the state. The Pao-wei Chü brings its case against the defendant, who may handle his own case or call upon someone else to do so. He is allowed to call as many witnesses as he likes.

"Cases of political prisoners are always tried like this, except in emergencies. 'Emergencies' are insurrections, mutinies or uprisings, when the Pao-wei Chü may arrest and punish leaders without delay or waiting for a court. This very seldom happens.

"In the Red Army itself there is a military court which handles cases involving prisoners who are soldiers. The Pao-wei Chü has no power inside the Red Army."

3 and 5. "The Pao-wei Chü itself does not have a large policing force. Each hsien has from one company to a platoon. For the provincial government and the Northwest government there are larger forces--security guards and special service guards as well. If these forces are insufficient, we have the Red Army to call upon. In the villages and district bureaus there are no security guards, but Peasant Red Guards (part-time volunteers) are used, when necessary, to enforce orders and judgments. They also do inspecting and policing work for the Pao-wei Chü."

4 and 6. "The difference between the Pao-wei Chü and the Kuomintang gendarmery or political police is this. The former only carries out the demands of the masses. No man is killed without mass approval and none is killed secretly, as is the Kuomintang practice. The people always know why.

"Another difference is that in some Kuomintang districts, if one man is convicted of political offense his whole family is arrested and even the children are killed, but the Soviet doesn't follow any such policy. One man's crime does not incriminate his family, relatives or friends. Neither their political nor economic rights are taken away from them.

"The third difference is found in the Soviet policy of pardoning political offenders. Those who respond to education and good treatment with good conduct are released, and their rights are restored.

"Fourth, prisoners are given exactly the same food as our own functionaries. They get the same clothes to wear. They are not beaten and tortured, as in Kuomintang jails.

"Today in Pao-an there was a trial of five men accused of organizing an anti-Soviet 'underground.' They were found guilty, and one was shot. Four others were given sentences of hard labor.

"These laborers are not put under guard (?--ES) but are formed into a company like the Red Army and are put under a commander* appointed by the Red Army, one of their own number. They do construction work, carry loads and such things, and get the same food and clothing as soldiers."

---

*I.e., a "trustee." Perhaps he meant no armed generals were necessary.

There are now no prisoners in Pao-an. The one who was held as a spy here in the summer has been released and returned to his home in Pao-an, according to Chou.* In all the soviet districts there are no more than sixty political prisoners at the present time (says Chou Hsing).

Chou Hsing continued:

"Thieves, robbers and ordinary criminals are very uncommon here. When any are arrested they are not imprisoned but are 'educated'--exposed to right ideas and social behavior. Sometimes they are given the choice of joining the Red Army or going to jail, but not often; it depends upon their conduct and the crime. When they are released, all their rights are restored. There is no discrimination against an ex-convict."

In answer to a direct question at this point, Chou Hsing said that from the time of the Kiangsi Red Army's arrival in North Shensi to date, the Pao-wei Chü had executed "fewer than twenty political prisoners." Counter-revolutionary killings** of Reds in the same period had "far exceeded" that number in this area.

---

*See p. 89.
**I.e., those captured by "White" forces.

VII.   THE AGITATION-PROPAGANDA BUREAU

1.   Wu Liang-p'ing 吳亮平 on Kiangsi

Wu Liang-p'ing interpreted in all my early talks with Mao Tse-tung
and in some other interviews in Pao-an. After my arrival in Pao-an
I sent to Yenching University for Wang Ju-mei 王汝梅 [Huang Hua
黃華] to come in to act as my interpreter with the consent of
Mao Tse-tung. Wang arrived in time to meet me at the front and he
worked as my interpreter during my later travels.

Wu Liang-p'ing was twenty-six when I met him, a red-cheeked youth with
a ready smile, an alert intelligence, and somthing of a reputation in
the party, already, as a Marxist theoretician. Mao obviously liked
him; so did other members of the Politburo. As Nym Wales wrote up
his biography in full in Inside Red China I need not amplify my notes
beyond the brief sketch of him which appeared in Red Star Over China.
I do not know his present position but I am rather surprised that he
has (apparently) not risen to top rank. He had a very "good" party
record inside and outside the Red areas.

The following notes are from an interview with Wu Liang-p'ing,
Secretary of the Agitation-Propaganda Bureau (Hsüan-ch'uan ku-tang
pu).

July 28, 1936. Pao-an. In answer to my question concerning activities
of his "bureau" Wu explained:

"Propaganda is devoted to informing, instructing and stimulating
people to action; agitation is for the purpose of organizing the emotion
and the revolutionary thinking created (stirred up) by propaganda. Without
propaganda Soviet policies cannot be fully explained and understood by the
people.

"In every party branch committee we have three bureaus (pu): agitation, propaganda, organization, and the women's section. Here in Shensi
many committees have a fourth: the Pai-ch'ü kung-shih pu (White Districts'
Work Bureau). In the Red Army political department there is also an agitation-propaganda section. In our agitation-propaganda work we use books
such as State and Revolution, The Proletarian Revolution and The Renegade
Kautsky, From February to October, Left Infantilism, and Stalin's Problems of
Leninism, Fundamentals of Leninism, On the Opposition, On the Third International. We use (or did use) a three-volume collection of articles and
resolutions about the Chinese revolution edited by the Central Committee of

the Chinese Communist Party and published in Juichin (Kiangsi) in 1933 (in Chinese called <u>Kuo-chi lien-hsien</u> [The Line of the International]); two books on Marxian political economy by 'Lapidos'; <u>Economic Geography</u>, by Palavin; a <u>Short History of the Russian Revolution</u>, by the Communist Party of the Soviet Union (<u>Wu-kuo ko-ming yü lien-pang kung-ch'an-tang chien-shih</u>, Juichin, 1933); and other Marxist and Leninist pamphlets on war and imperialism.

"Among books on warfare published in Kiangsi were the following: <u>Political Work in the Red Army</u> (<u>Hung-chün chung ti cheng-chih kung-tso</u>, Juichin, 1932); <u>The Mixed (United?) Army of Germany</u> (<u>Te-kuo lien-ho ping-chün</u>, Juichin, 1933); <u>Staff Work in the Red Army</u> (<u>Hung-chün chung ti ts'an-mou kung-tso</u>, Juichin, 1934); <u>On Guerrilla Warfare</u> (<u>Yo-chi chan-cheng wen-t'i</u> [Problems of guerrilla warfare?], Juichin, 1934); and many others on tactics, as well as pamphlets on strategy, tactics, etc.

"Other publications printed at Juichin, Kiangsi, included <u>Character of the Economic Structure</u>, by Lo Fu, in 1934 (<u>Chung-kuo ching-chi hsing-chih wen-t'i-ti yen-chiu</u>); <u>Program of the Comintern</u> (<u>Kung-ch'an kuo-chi kang-ling</u>, 1933); <u>On the Colonial Resolution</u> (<u>Chih-min-ti ko-ming</u>, 1933); <u>On the National Revolution</u>, by Marx, Lenin, Stalin, 1933; <u>A Brief Explanation of the Constitution of the Soviet Union</u> (<u>Su-lien hsien-fa chien-shih</u>, 1934); <u>Political Work in the Red Army in Wartime</u> (<u>Chan-shih cheng-chih kung-tso</u>, 1934); <u>On the Chinese Army</u>, by a 'Russian Comrade' (??), (<u>Chung-kuo ti chün-tai</u>, 1934).

"Also published in 1934: <u>Archives of the Second Congress</u> (?), by Mao Tse-tung (<u>Erh-tz'u ta-hui fen-chun</u>); <u>Collection of Revolutionary Poems</u> (<u>Ko-ming shih-chi</u>); <u>A Collection of Revolutionary Cartoons</u> (<u>Ko-ming hua-chi</u>); <u>Collection of Revolutionary Songs</u> (<u>Ko-ming ko-chi</u>); <u>Collection of Folk Songs</u> (<u>Min-ko-chi</u>), all at Juichin. We also published many textbooks for Red Army troops and for ordinary schools. Po Ku and Lo Fu wrote articles which were collected in books.

"Periodicals: <u>Struggle</u> (<u>Tou-cheng</u>), a weekly edited by Lo Fu 洛甫 [pseudonym of Wang Chia-hsiang 王稼祥], early 1933 to the present (1936), circulation 8,000, one copper; <u>Red China</u> (<u>Hung-se Chung-hua</u>), a newspaper for the general population, organ of the Soviet government, tabloid size, begun in Kiangsi in 1932, had a circulation of more than 50,000, still published in mimeograph here; <u>Young Truth</u> (<u>Ch'ing-nien shih-hua</u>), organ

of the Young Communist League, circulation 15,000 in Kiangsi, published
1932-35, now suspended; Youth Knowledge (Ch'ing-nien chih-shih), still
published periodically; Red Star (Hung-hsing), had circulation of 20,000,
1933-34; Soviet Worker (Su-ch'u kung-jen), a weekly, 3,000-4,000, 1933-34,
discontinued during the Long March; Be Prepared (Shih-k'o chun-pei che),
circulation 4,000, 1933-34 in Kiangsi, now halted. All the foregoing were
printed in the three Soviet government printing and publishing houses:
Central Publishing House (Chung-yang ch'u-pan chü), Military Committee
Publishing House (Chün-wei yu-su shu-chü), and the Young Truth Printing
Works (Ch'ing-nien shih-hua yin-shu so).

"There were many lithographing (handicraft printers) firms besides
the large houses. The Military Council had one, and the provincial party
committees had others. Mimeographed publications were also numerous. The
army corps had their own publications, and armies within corps had newspapers
about soldiers' lives, their exploits, courage, heroism, etc. To be mentioned
in the army press was a great honor.

"Decorations awarded Red Army fighters in Kiangsi included the follow-
ing: First Class Order of the Red Star (gold); Second Class Order of the
Red Star (gold and silver); Third Class Order of the Red Star (silver).
More than ten (but less than twenty) top Communists had received the First
Class Order of the Red Star."

2. On the Bureau's Work

Wu spoke enthusiastically and nostalgically--as a southerner--of the
work of agitation and propaganda in the south. He tended to despair of doing
as well in Shensi; the human material certainly seemed far poorer to start
with.

"Agitation was a powerful weapon in our hands, to mobilize (recruit)
people for the Red Army. We raised recruiting slogans everywhere and were
amazingly successful. In a recruiting drive from May 1933 to October 1934,
we brought in about 100,000 new soldiers. In May and June alone we recruited
more than 60,000. In 1934 we 'mobilized' 700,000 piculs of rice in donations
and loans. This collection was preceded by widespread propaganda, extensive

meetings called by all soviets, all workers, all peasants, and all party organizations, over a period of two months. At the end of this campaign the quota was achieved. This was accomplished entirely without military coercion. No soldiers were stationed in the villages and towns.

"In every village there is a communist nucleus, and one man is responsible for Red Guard and Vanguard work. Red Guards are enlisted from males between twenty-three and forty-five years old. Young Vanguards are between sixteen and twenty-three. Most of them are not party members, but the Vanguards are led by the Young Communist League, and the Red Guards are organized and led by the Communist party.

"Every Red Army division has an agitation-propaganda group of ten or more, and there is a representative in the regiment or small groups. They are responsible for the drama groups--for providing plays, operas, 'sings,' ballet, to spread propaganda. Each corps has its drama group. Even in the platoon, the political director has the duty of doubling as agitation-propaganda leader and organizes games and contests among the men."

3. On Policy toward "White" Captives

"Officers and soldiers captured are first given instruction and invited to join the Red Army. If they choose to leave they are allowed to do so; they carry literature and new ideas about the Reds to the outside. For example, Liu Teh-yu 劉德裕 (?) chief of staff of the 109th Manchurian Division, was so indoctrinated by Soviet propaganda and then released. ('Don't print this,' said Wu). In fact our best propagandists are White officers and soldiers who have been captured [indoctrinated--E.S.] and then released. Last New Year we gave a big feast at Wang-ya-pao to White officers of Chang Hsüeh-liang's army. They were amazed when Mao and Chou En-lai attended. This policy toward officers had never been applied before-- although in Kiangsi we had used it toward ordinary soldiers. But it was in (only after we reached) Shensi that we applied it to officers.

"As for international propaganda, little has been done so far. We have not been able to reach the outside world, and news of our activities is incomplete and scarce. We do have a news-gathering organization here called the Red China News Agency, which has correspondents in all important places (?)."

VIII. COMMUNIST YOUTH ORGANIZATION

Data supplied by Feng Wen-pin 馮文彬 , Communist Youth Corps
secretary, Pao-an, Shensi, July 25, 1936.

1. History of the Communist Youth Corps

Hui Tsin-yung [Yün Tai-ying 惲代英 ?], Chang T'ai-lei 張太雷 ,
Hsiao Ch'u-nü 蕭楚女 , Shih Ts'un-t'ung 施存統 and four others
founded the Communist Youth Corps in May 1920. It was at first called
Socialist Youth. At that meeting it was decided to affiliate with the
Shao-kung kuo-chi--Communist Youth International. (Socialist Youth had
existed before 1918). A second meeting was called in August 1923. The
Socialist Youth was limited then to student and cultural circles. At
this second meeting the policy was changed to provide for organizing on
a wider scale, also to determine relations between Socialist Youth and
the Communist party. In 1924 the Communist Youth Central Committee called
an enlarged meeting and it was proposed that the Communist Youth should
be "proletarianized." At the Third Representative Meeting, held in Canton,
February 1925, it was agreed that the Communist party program should be
followed. The Socialist Youth turned to labor and the mass movement.
The slogan "Communist Youth must be proletarianized" was adopted, and the
name was changed to Communist Youth of China.

In August 1927, the Fourth Representative Meeting was called secretly
in Wuhan, where resolutions were adopted condeming Chen Tu-hsiu's "opportunism" and Communist cooperation with the Kuomintang. In the same year a fifth
Communist Youth meeting was held (just after the Fifth Congress of the
Chinese Communist Party). A new position was adopted in line with resolutions of the party. After the fifth meeting, during 1930, the Communist
Youth was abolished and became instead a department of the Communist party.
This was under the leadership of Li Li-san. Following this crisis and the
fourth meeting of the Central Committee, Chinese Communist Party, the
Communist Youth was revived in the Soviet districts and the Red Army. From
then till now there has been no All-China meeting of the Chinese Youth.

The following people served as secretary of the Communist Youth in the order named:

Shih Ts'un-t'ung	施存統	Wang Yung-sheng	王永生
Chang T'ai-lei	張太雷	Hu Chün-ho	胡均鶴
Jen Pi-shih	任弼時	Ku Tso-lin	顧作霖
Kuan Hsiang-ying	關向應	K'ai Feng	凱丰
Wang Ju-ch'eng	王儒程	[pseudonym of Ho K'o-ch'üan	
Yuan Ping-hui	袁炳輝	何克全]	
		Feng Wen-pin	馮文彬

Members of the Communist Youth Central Committee (1936): K'ai Feng, Wang Shen-ping, Po Ku, Ch'en Ch'ang-hao, Lu Ting-yi, Kuan Hsiang-ying, Wang Ju-ch'eng, Huang Lien-yi (imprisoned, student), Feng Wen-pin, Liu Ying, Hu Yao-pang, Ch'en Shih-fa, Pai Tse-ming, Li Jei-shan, Kao Lan-shan.

2. Activities

There are three branches of the Communist Youth: Communist Youth for Red Army Expansion; Communist Youth in the Red Army; and Communist Youth in Soviet Construction.

a. Communist Youth for Red Army Expansion (Kung-tang k'uo ta Hung-chün 共党擴大紅軍)

In Kiangsi in 1933 this organization recruited 60,000 youths for the Red Army, in 1934 about 100,000 members. Of this total about one-third were Communist Youth members. The Communist Youth had brigades in this work in all Soviet districts in the south.

In Kiangsi the "Communist Youth International" was organized, consisting of 8,000 Red Army soldiers affiliated with world communist youth directly. One whole division (the Fifteenth) consisted of Communist Youths. The Communist Youth always mobilized its own youth to comfort and cheer the Fifteenth as its own. Division headquarters had relations directly with the Communist Youth Central. Committee Brigade headquarters were under the Communist Youth provincial committee. The Communist Youth produced many Red Army heroes. Under the Communist Youth were these three organizations:

Communist Youth (members age 16 to 23); Young Vanguards (age 14 to 16); Youth Brigades (age 8 to 14).

Examples of Communist Youth "heroes." During the "Million Iron Red Army Movement" in Chang-ting-hsien (Fukien), the branch Communist Youth secretary, Wang Sheng-ting, and a group leader, Wang Ching-t'ing, led the entire Young Vanguard organization (thirty-two) in the village of Chou-t'ien to enlist in the Red Army.

In Nan-kuan-hsien, Kiangsi, Comrade Wang K'o-sheng led seventy-five persons to join the Red Army. In the same province, in Kan-hsien, a young communist leader named Ch'en Cheng-liu led fifty-eight persons to join the army. In Ningtu, in Kiangsi, the Communist Youth secretary, Hsieh Yen-p'ing, recruited more than three hundred youths for the army.

In Chiang-hsien (renamed Kung-lüeh-hsien in memory of Huang Kung-lüeh 黃 公 畧) a woman named Li Lo-ying persuaded her husband to join the Red Army. In Yu Tu, Kiangsi, a woman named Hsiao Yu-chun divorced her husband because he would not join. Another girl in the same place persuaded her husband to join the Red Army by insisting that their marriage would have no future under the White armies (if the Kuomintang won). In one case in Juichin, in a family of eight brothers, all were recruited by the Communist Youth for the Red Army. Many hundreds of cases like this were reported in the "Report of the Communist Youth Central Committee in China to the Communist Youth International in China" before the Seventh Congress, 1934, Juichin, Kiangsi.

b. Communist Youth in the Red Army

About forty per cent of Red Army men are under twenty-three. Of these about half are Communist Youth members. In the Red Army a special organization of youth called the Hsiao Tui is active in every company and every brigade. Its main task is educational. In addition to regular Red Army classroom work, the Communist Youth organizes special lectures, teaches songs and dramatics, dancing (sic), etc. It maintains Lenin Corners, down to battalion level, and holds at least two meetings monthly to discuss Communist Youth problems. Under the supervision of a political director it leads discussions on social

problems like sex, marriage, work, etc. Communist Youth also gives men
supplementary military training: how to get cover in air raids, marksman-
ship, camouflage, how to spot enemy officers in battle, boxing, calisthenics,
athletics of various kinds, basket ball, etc.

Maximum membership of Communist Youth in Kiangsi soviets was about
400,000, both in and out of the army. Membership dues, 1 copper a month.

Communist Youth leaders especially emphasize literacy training. Lenin
Corners offer regular daily courses in character-recognition. In each company a Young Communist is delegated to teach others, on the march. He carries
a sharp stick, if paper is lacking, and uses this to scratch characters into
the ground or into a box of sand which is sometimes carried for the purpose.
When encamped, "wall newspapers" in Lenin rooms are written by the men, each
making his own contribution, practicing characters and reporting. The aim is
to get everybody to try.

Public health is another concern of the Communist Youth, which teaches
the Red Army to obey the "Three Oughts and the Three Noughts" and teach the
people. The "Oughts": observe discipline; be clean; be polite. The "Noughts":
don't drink wine; don't smoke; don't drink cold (unboiled) water.

The Communist Youth gives soldiers and recruits instruction in first
aid and teaches not only remedies for common illnesses but how to avoid them.
Lectures on health are given at night. The Communist Youth enforces health
measures when the Red Army builds latrines.

During rests and in encampments the Communist Youth drama groups put
on sings, dramas, slogan-shoutings.

Communist Youth meetings are called every five to seven days, when the
army is not fighting, to discuss practical problems of leadership, morale,
combatting any defeatist tendencies, contact with world youth, and so on.
They discuss recent battles: who was most brave and who was most awkward,
and why. They talk about shoes, about new uniforms, about their families.
During a march the Communist Youth helps enforce discipline and vigilance,
being on the lookout for anyone tending to be slack. They criticize officers,
food, cooking, quarters, objectionable orders; they may ask for explanations
of everything. The Communist Youth brings soldiers news of their families
and villages. They help soldiers write letters home; at home they help

parents and wives to write their loved ones, and to send them gifts.

Any soldier dissatisfied with a superior officer may write to the higher officer above him and criticize and even demand his removal. The Communist Youth will transmit the complaint and help investigate the charges. Most such problems are solved within the battalion. Sometimes the whole battalion holds a mass meeting to consider charges, if several make the same criticism. Officers are sometimes dismissed by a majority vote; it is rare, but has happened.

c. Communist Youth in Soviet Construction

Communist Youth in the rear helps solve problems of relationships between apprentices and masters, between herdsmen and shepherds, husbands and wives, children and their oppressors. The work of the apprentice is long, hard, poorly paid or not paid at all. The Communist Youth helps apprentices win shorter hours, less work, and work on a contract basis, at first by persuasion, later by law.

Saturday Brigades are organized by the Communist Youth and Youth Vanguards and the Youth Brigades to collect manure, reclaim wasteland, help in sowing and harvesting. Women and girls are mobilized for special group tasks, under the slogan: "You do the work at the front; we'll do the work in the rear." Formerly no women worked in the fields in Shensi; now even "bound feet" can be seen tilling. Young Communist groups encourage peasants to plant vegetables, and they themselves plant vegetables in wasteland—mostly corn and potatoes.

IX. CHOU EN-LAI 周恩来

1. On Chiang Kai-shek

For two days I lived in a cave next door to Chou En-lai in Pai-chia-p'ing, Shensi, while he talked and prepared me for an itinerary which he suggested would give me a fair picture of territory under Communist rule. Pai-chia-p'ing was then the Red outpost nearest to Sian; it was a communications and transportation center, with a manually operated military radio, and a courier depot. The Red "capital" (Pao-an) was a day's journey farther west. The notes which follow were not used in Red Star Over China because, when I was writing that book, after the Sian Incident occurred, Chou sent a message to me at Peking begging me to refrain from quoting him. As a result of that Incident and its settlement, a liaison headquarters had been set up by the Reds in Sian, and Chou made responsible for conducting negotiations with Chiang Kai-shek. He feared he would be embarrassed in this task if I quoted his remarks. That is rather interesting because it may indicate that at the time he spoke to me Chou and the Communists did not conceive of a United Front which could include Chiang, but only of one which would result from defections from Chiang to the United Front to be formed against both Chiang and Japan.

As I wrote quite fully what I know of Chou En-lai and his wife, Teng Ying-ch'ao in an article for the Saturday Evening Post, in 1954, I omit biographical notes here.

July 9, 1936. Pai-chia-p'ing.

Edgar Snow: "What were the chief reasons for the success of the counter-revolution of 1927, and what were the chief mistakes of the Communists?"

Chou En-lai: "Our first mistake unquestionably was in not deepening the revolution among the peasantry, especially in Kwangtung and Kwangsi, where peasants were already armed. Our party followed an opportunistic policy in this respect, expanding horizontally (in numbers) instead of vertically (organizing fighters directly from the peasantry).

"Secondly, we failed to develop the necessary revolutionary leadership among cadres of the Kuomintang army. We let slip out of our grasp many good officers who could have been won over to our side. In 1926 it would still have been possible for us to enlist and equip ten divisions of Communist troops had we energetically sought to do so.

"Thirdly, we threw away our chance to hold hegemony of the Kuomintang, then still a revolutionary party, by mistakes in tactics.* A single example:

---

*An almost identical mistake was made by the Communist Party of Burma in 1945.

in Shanghai we failed to take advantage of contradictions which then existed both in the Kuomintang and among the imperialists. We lost the hegemony of the Kuomintang which was rightfully ours. It was ours for the taking after March 1926, had we pursued correct tactics. All rightists had been driven temporarily out of power; the leftist Wang Ching-wei 汪精衛 was cooperating closely with us; Chiang Kai-shek, then a centrist, was isolated. Had Communists entered into the Kuomintang in full force and struggled for hegemony, instead of remaining outside, we could have formed a coalition with the Left Wing and secured and held the leadership.* The army, the merchants, the students, even overseas Chinese, then agreed with our main tactical program.

"Again, during Chiang's march on Shanghai, there was still time to organize a coalition against him and the rightists. The majority of the military leadership was still outside his hands. In the Northern Expedition were the Second, Fourth, Seventh and Eighth armies, all of which were outside Chiang's control. He had only three divisions, and they were the least dependable of all."

Q. "How do you explain such mistakes or miscalculations?"

A. "They were due to several things. First, the lack of experience and Marxist tradition in China; our party was only a few years old. Second, leadership was divided in the party itself between Chen Tu-hsiu, a petty-bourgeois mentality, and the younger, just-emerging groups with a thorough understanding of Marxism. Third, to the uneven development of the revolution in different parts of the country among different groups. Fourth, to the lack of proletarian organization and experience and to the success of the petty-bourgeois elements in maintaining supremacy in the party."

Q. "What book do you regard as the best account of this period of the revolution?"

A. "Chung-kuo ke-ming chi-pen wen-ti,** written by one of our members in Kiangsi. There are mistakes in it, of fact and of analysis, but it is the best thing yet prepared."

---

*Implicit criticism of Comintern directives and tactical leadership?
** English title: **Fundamental Questions of the Chinese Revolution.**

Q. "Are you optimistic about present prospects?"

A. "There is no doubt that the Chinese revolution is now nearing another high point. It will probably come to power on the vehicle of the anti-Japanese movement. Its success or failure in the near future depends upon the development of the mass movement and how the mass as a generating power is organized against Japanese imperialism. Food and land remain the primary demands of the revolutionary peasantry, but after that is the question of national resistance to Japan. The peasants' enthusiastic welcome of the Red Army during its Shansi (1935) expedition was due largely to ready acceptance of this (anti-Japanese) slogan."

Q. "Do you consider Chiang's position now stronger or weaker than it was several years ago?"

A. "Chiang Kai-shek reached the zenith of his power in 1934 and he is now rapidly going down. During his Fifth War in Kiangsi he was able to mobilize 500,000 troops for attack and blockade; it was his period of greatest power. When he had destroyed the Ninteenth Route Army and forced us to withdraw, he was supreme in the Yangtze Valley. But all this was achieved at terrific cost, and since then his civil war slogans have lost all appeal. At the last Kuomintang congress he dared not use anti-Red slogans, because of fear of being criticized."

Chou argued that Chiang was more and more dividing his forces by attempting to spread to all the frontiers; he was everywhere weakening himself by this. "His lack of ability to concentrate is now his weakness." He had committed himself too broadly in terms of his real political consolidation. Chou went on:

"If he allows the Red Army to build a base in the Northwest it will ultimately prove impossible for him to make any such concentration against us, such as he made in Kiangsi. And yet he cannot now prevent the development of such a base, nor of its rapid expansion and consolidation.

"The second point to remember is that if the anti-Japanese movement develops he will almost certainly be deprived of his dictatorship (lose dictatorial control). His forces are neither so big, so concentrated nor so loyal as at the time of his fifth anti-Red war. In the event of a Japanese conflict, the anti-Japanese forces (i.e., the Red Army) will detach important parts of his command. The first day of the anti-Japanese war, as Chiang well

knows, will put a stamp of doom on his hegemony. It is not necessary to
enumerate the generals and troops of the national armies where this defection will first occur. However, it is well known that Ch'en Ch'eng 陳誠 ,
one of his ablest commanders, has little enthusiasm for the anti-Red war.
Hu Tsung-nan 胡宗南 has even less. Both are former Left students at
Whampoa and are former comrades of many Red Army leaders. Both are patriotic.
Neither can be relied upon by Chiang much longer to carry on his personal
war against the Reds. In the event of war against Japan, both would almost
certainly support the United Front."

Q. "What is your opinion of Chiang as a military man?"

A. "Not so much (high?). As a tactician he is a bungling amateur.
As a strategist he is perhaps better.

"As a tactician Chiang follows the style of Napoleon. Napoleonic
tactics depend tremendously on the high morale and fighting spirit of the
troops, on the will to victory. It is there that Chiang always makes his
mistakes; he likes too much to fancy himself the dashing hero leading fight-
to-the death troops. Whenever he leads a regiment or division he makes a
mess of it. He always concentrates his men and attempts to take a position
by storming it. In the Wuhan (1927) battle he led a division up to the city
after others had failed, and threw its whole strength against the enemy's
defense works. His division was smashed to pieces.

"At Nanchang he repeated that error. He made an assault on that city,
held by Sun Chuan-fang 孫傳芳 , and used his own first division,
refusing to wait for reinforcements. Sun withdrew and let Chiang enter
part of the town, then counter-attacked and drove Chiang's forces into a
trap between the city wall and river. They were lost. Chiang had the
First, Second and Twenty-first Divisions with him but he used only the
First. Yeh Chien-ying (now chief-of-staff of the Eastern Front Red Army)
at that time commanded the Twenty-first Division. Chiang's stupidity
disgusted him, and he left his command shortly afterward.

"During the recent Shansi campaign Chiang ordered General Ch'en
Ch'eng to send two divisions against the Reds and annihilate them. Ch'en,
a better tactician, declined to do so, fearing an ambush. We intercepted
his reply to Chiang Kai-shek. We would indeed have welcomed such a concentration; in just this kind of attack we disarmed 6,000 of Chang Hsüeh-

liang's troops last December (1935). Fortunately for Nanking, Chiang does not often take personal command at the front. Among other reasons he doesn't is that he cannot ride a horse.

"But Chiang is a better strategist than tactician. He has better political sense than military, and that is how he wins over other warlords. He often plans a campaign in its entirety with considerable skill."

Q. "Whom do you consider Nanking's ablest field commanders?"

A. "Ch'en Ch'eng is a good steady plugger, but there's nothing brilliant about him. Hu Tsung-nan is probably Chiang's ablest commander. He has done the most effective fighting against the Reds. Ho Ying-ch'in 何應欽 was formerly not a bad commander, but in 1927 he was severely defeated (by Sun Ch'uan-fang?) and badly frightened and lost his fighting spirit and has never been of any use (in the field) since then."

Q. "From a military standpoint, what were the main reasons for the defeat of the Red Army in the Fifth Campaign in Kiangsi?"

A. "Two important factors led to Chiang Kai-shek's first success. First he adopted, on German advice, the system of building blockhouses in depth, and limiting his advances to short attacks and consolidations, ending in gradual effective encirclement by superior forces (500,000 Kuomintang troops versus 100,000 Red regulars). Second, our failure to cooperate militarily with the Fukien rebellion led by the Nineteenth Route (Kuomintang) Army and support it as an important diversion. We could have successfully cooperated with Fukien, but due to the advice of Li Teh (the Reds' German adviser) and the advisory group in Shanghai we withdrew instead, and delivered an attack against Chiang Kai-shek's concentrations near Juichin. This enabled Chiang Kai-shek to turn the Nineteenth Route Army's flank and destroy them."

2. Shensi and Kiangsi

Chou En-lai said:

"Peasants in Shensi are extremely poor, their land very unproductive. If Kiangsi peasants owned as much land as Shensi peasants, they would be considered rich landlords. The Red arsenal in Kiangsi turned out 500,000 shells (bullets?) per month; here we make very few. Kiangsi also made hand

grenades in quantity; Shensi's production is very low. The population of
the Kiangsi soviet numbered 3,000,000, whereas here it is at most 600,000
(in parts of three provinces). In Kiangsi and Fukien people brought bundles
with them when they joined the Red Army; here they do not even bring chop-
sticks; they are utterly destitute.

"Two large settlements in the Yen-ch'ih area (Salt Lake hsien) on the
Suiyuan border have just been captured by the Red Army. Here the land has
been owned for nearly a hundred years by the French and Belgian fathers.
Their holdings total about 500 square li. Their ownership traces back to
the murder of two priests by a band of Mongols, nearly a century ago. Today
the only houses seen on all this vast stretch of farmland surrounding the
lake are owned by the Church. There are about thirty churches and chapels
in the area, and many rich vineyards. The Mongols come there for water and
wine and use the pastures.

"When we came into this area we made a treaty with the priests leaving
the church undisturbed in temporary possession of its property, and guarantee-
ing religious freedom, while in turn the priests promised to share food and
wealth with the state, to observe soviet law, and not to propagandize the
Red troops. This treaty has been fairly kept. The priests agreed to publish
a statement to the world, and especially to all Catholic fathers in the
Church in China, calling upon them to join the United Front and oppose
Japanese imperialism. They are reported to be sincerely anti-fascist and
are influenced by the People's-Front victory in France. They sent a telegram for us (the Reds) to congratulate the French on their People's-Front
victory."

3. On Future Plans

July 10, 1936. Pai-chia-p'ing.
Chou said:
"Two possible strategic plans are open to the Red Army now. Both
await the union of our troops from the south (under Chu Teh, Ho Lung, and
Chang Kuo-t'ao 張國燾,) with P'eng Teh-huai's and Mao Tse-tung's
forces here. This will take place in late July or early August, in south
Kansu. It will be a reunion after a year of separation. Last year when

Mao and P'eng [and Chou] started toward Shensi, the Central Committee's plan to expand in the Northwest was opposed by Chang Kuo-t'ao. He insisted on remaining in Szechwan and attempting to establish a base there and then return southward. However, Mao and others knew that fortifications were already being built behind them and that heavy reinforcements of government troops had poured into Kweichow and Hunan. They believed any attempt to return to a southern base would meet with failure. The Central Committee's decision was still in dispute when Nanking troops began to attack in the Mou-kung area and drove a wedge between two sections of the army. Chu Teh and Chang Kuo-t'ao were cut off from the others, the Red Army divided into two sections. Chu Teh was not in sympathy with Chang, but as his army was behind Chang's forces he was caught [captured?] by him. Now after one year Chang has agreed to the Northwest plan and admitted his mistakes. Taking advantage of the (disturbed) Southwest situation, which diverted many Nanking troops from Szechwan, he is moving into Kansu. When a meeting is effected, a conference will be called to discuss two strategic plans, as follows:

"First: To expand southward and eastward into southern Kansu, reaching toward Honan, where the Red Army would seek to set up a strong Soviet base for action against both Nanking and Japan, if necessary. It would also provide a focus for the rallying of all peripheral, potentially anti-Nanking, anti-Japanese forces, pivoting perhaps on T'ung-kuan. Whether Chang Hsüeh-liang would join the Reds in this movement, which would take place under anti-Japanese slogans, is not known, but it is a possibility. Depending upon an assessment of combined Red Army strength, upon popular support for the United Front, and upon the general political situation at the time of the merger, either this plan will be followed, or:

"Second: Efforts will be made to come rapidly into direct contact with the Japanese by penetrating Suiyuan and Inner Mongolia. This movement would involve some war against the Moslem warlords of Ninghsia and Kansu and attempts to win over the Mongol princes of Inner Mongolia, as well as to win the masses to support an anti-Japanese front. It would mean a drive against Fu Tso-yi in Suiyuan, penetration of Outer Mongolia, and establishment of a line of communications between Red China and Sinkiang. This course would enable the Reds to form a base strong enough for an independent campaign against Japan, in case the political situation favors it."

In a conversation I had with the German adviser, Li Teh ("Otto"), on September 29, about the above two concepts, Li Teh expressed the opinion that the Red Army would move westward, above Lanchow in Kansu, and attempt to take Ninghsia city. This "would not happen for another two months," in all probablity. By then the three main army corps would have been united, rested, reorganized and given new training. This comment may be of interest chiefly as an indication that the Reds were then—before the Sian Incident—thinking mainly in terms of falling back on the northwest and northern Chinese frontiers abutting on Soviet territory.

The foregoing interviews were in English, of which Chou had a halting but intelligible command. I made notes and wrote them up in full, read them back to Chou, corrected or clarified and helped him find elusive words, then made a revised draft from which this is quoted.

X. THE LIU HSIAO 劉曉 STORY

<u>September 1936</u>. <u>Headquarters Yu Wang Pao, Ninghsia</u>.

Liu Hsiao, chairman of the political department of the First Front
Army, was born in Shenking, Hunan, in 1911, in a family of "middle landlords." His father had studied in Japan two years and he returned "modernized"
—but "backward all the same." He taught Liu not to worship idols, but he
was not advanced in other ways. Liu Hsiao began school at the age of five;
his father was the teacher. He was severe with his son and punished him for
the most trivial offenses. When Liu Hsiao was six his father took a second
wife, who was cruel to the boy.

"She made me carry water in heavy buckets, although we had servants
to do that. When I accidentally tore my clothes she said that I had done
so purposely, and beat me. She told my father I was a 'useless thing' and
not worth raising. My grandmother was kind to me, however. She lived with
us and tried to placate my stepmother without success.

"In school I worked hard and led my class. The teachers loved me very
much. I did not study the classics and never read the Four Books, but at the
age of seven I could write poems. From the first I studied in the technical,
or so-called Westernized, schools. As I became a good student my father
treated me with more kindness. After four years in primary school I entered
higher primary, where I didn't do so well, as my father wasn't there to
control me. I liked to fight. I was nicknamed Liu Po-wang, after the bandit
leader of the district, who had been executed four years earlier. By the
end of the third term I was at the bottom of the class. My teacher, a kindly
man who spoke to me sympathetically, asked me to improve. After that I
reformed for some time.

"When I was ten my teacher organized a 'Save China Society' and asked
me to join. I organized several groups called Chiu-kuo-hui Propaganda Corps.
It was our duty to awaken people. I was assigned to talk to some bandits
about sixty <u>li</u> from our school, and my teacher and I went to see them. They
received me politely and agreed that it was our duty to save China. They
called a meeting where I spoke. They were very much impressed. 'So small
a child knows how to save the country but we do nothing,' they said. 'We
must take up some responsibility.'

"We stayed there for four days. The bandits finally decided to give up their career of crime and robbery. My teacher arranged for them to join the military force. On my return my father threatened to disown me if I ever repeated such an action. I said I knew nothing of the danger but only knew the country was being lost. When he heard how the bandits had behaved he, too, was moved, and he relented. Some years later that teacher became a Communist and was killed during the Great Revolution.

"A year after that I graduated from higher primary school and my step-mother wanted me to go to work. But our economic condition was good; it was not necessary for me to earn money, and my father argued that I would earn more if I graduated from middle school. So I was sent to the Chao Yang school, run by the American Christian Reformed Church, located in Sheng-choufu.

"At the door of the new school I was met by the principal, J. Frank Booker, who said he would have to examine me. He held his ear and said, 'What is this?' in English. I had only learned the alphabet and did not understand him. He then said the examination was over; I did not know English, so I would have to enter primary school. My first English teacher could not speak Chinese; I sat all day listening without understanding. After a month I had another examination, and got zero. Booker called me for an interview and said I would have to enter first grade, primary school, unless I had made progress by the end of the next month. During that month I stayed up till midnight and got up before daybreak, all to study English. After two months I caught up with the English class. At the end of the term I spent my vacation studying English. After one year in higher primary school I was allowed to enter middle school.

"In middle school I studied the Bible and believed; I became a Christian. I worked earnestly for the church, even preaching in the streets on Saturdays and Sundays. I became a member of the YMCA.

"The next year a Chinese preacher named Li came from Nanking. He was a progressive Christian with political ideas. He said that the Bible should not be read literally. The world was not made in seven days, though it evolved in seven ages. He said that if you did not read the Bible in accordance with a scientific understanding of history it was a meaningless story.

He was interested in the student movement and told me something of the May Thirtieth Incident.

"In the same town there was a Catholic priest, an American, whom we frequently went to see. He was a kind and intelligent man, and it was enjoyable to discuss things with him. He explained to us the differences between Catholicism and Protestantism. Gradually we lost all belief in superstitions, but we still clung to the principles of Christianity.

"Next year a friend of mine who was in the Hunan Normal School came to visit me, but he refused to come inside the building. He said this was not China; it was imperialist territory. I had forgotten my country and become a foreign slave, he said. He talked to me for a long time, made me see the pitiful political condition of China, and asked me to leave the school to help save the country. I was much affected. I did begin to see a connection between missionaries and imperialism.

"In the Eighth Middle School, a government school nearby, students had Saturday afternoon and Sunday free; we were confined and had to attend chapel on Sunday. I opposed this and proposed at a YMCA meeting that we demand a change. Students who agreed with me delegated me to speak to the principal, who refused to grant our request. We went on strike the next Sunday and seven of us were dismissed. When I returned home my father disowned me (again) and refused to put me in any other school. My uncle, however, persuaded my father to give me $300, and I went to Nanking to enter school there.

"I went from Chengteh to Changsha on a steamer across Tungt'ing Lake, so big that we lost sight of land. I became homesick and longed to turn back. My place beside the engine room was hot; I felt the fires of hell for three days. In Hankow I saw my first Indian policeman, who was so tall I started running as soon as he looked at me. Thinking I was a thief he chased me, caught me, and took me to the police station. Everyone laughed when I told my story; I was released.

"At Nanking I saw the Reverend Li, who introduced me to some of his friends. I stayed with my uncle, who was a teacher, a radical, a socialist and a revolutionary. He gave me A New Conception of Society to read, and the ABC of Communism, New Youth, and The Guide, a communist magazine. I read books by Yü Ta-fu, and felt sentimental and romantic also. A friend came to advise me and give some clarification. He urged me to join an organization and struggle for a new society.

"I stayed half a year in Nanking and talked many times to my friend. When my money was almost gone I went to Shanghai and . . . returned with only five dollars in my pocket. My father sent me some money so that I could enter school in Shanghai. I entered the Political Science Institute at Wusung, but I lasted only half a year there before I was dismissed as a suspected Red.

"Next I lived for a while in the French concession. I joined the Communist party finally in 1926 and was given party work to do. I helped organize the Shanghai uprising. After the counter-revolution I hid in a small room in Shanghai for one month, afraid to go out. Many of my comrades were killed at that time. When I re-established contact with the party I was sent to Feng-hsien, north of the Yangtze, where I taught in a combined primary-middle school and worked among students and farmers. Most of the teachers there were Young Communists or Communists. Soon the school was completely revolutionized. We used to sing the 'International' and the 'Red Flag' at school, and we threw away Kuomintang textbooks and used only communist books. Most of the students joined the Communist party or Communist Youth. Many peasant organizations were set up. In due course we were attacked by Kuomintang troops, and most of the teachers and many of the students fled, some to become partisans, others to work as secret organizers in the city.

"After three months I was sent to work among the salt workers in Pootung, along the sea. I worked there long enough to set up a large party branch among all salt workers. We were able to lead a local uprising there but were soon put down by the Kuomintang.

"After these experiences I hid in Shanghai, but in June of 1928 I was captured by the French police. My 'office' was searched and some secret papers were discovered. I was put in jail and held there a year and two months. When I came out in 1929 I worked in the provincial committee but I was soon again arrested by International Settlement police and imprisoned in the Ward Road jail. Kuomintang authorities demanded my extradition and I was sent to Lunghua prison. There I was kept till 1931. After my release I hid, and later the party smuggled me to the Soviet district in Fukien, where I became secretary of the provincial committee. I was there two years; then I was transferred to the Central Soviet district, where most of my work was in the provincial committee of South Kiangsi.

"After the Fifth Extermination Campaign I made the Long March with the Red Army to the Northwest and was assigned to my present post."

XI. MAO TSE-TUNG 毛澤東

1. A Few Asides (Return to Shensi: 1939)

I returned to Yenan in late September 1939, two weeks' after the
outbreak of World War II. Chou En-lai had flown to Moscow, ostensibly
to seek increased aid for China, and presumably to get a reorientation
on Stalinist policy since the Nazi-Soviet Pact. I had two official
interviews in which questions and answers were written down and translated and re-translated by Wang Ju-mei 王汝梅 (?)(now known as
Huang Hua 黄華), a former Yenching student and a youth leader
from Peking, whom I had brought to Pao-an in 1936.* Prior to the
formal interviews I visited Mao for dinner one evening and had some
casual off-the-record discussion, on the basis of which I wrote the
diary notes recorded below.

September 23, 1939. I found Mao living in a "modern" three-room cave
"apartment" in the loess hills a few li outside Yenan. I noticed again the
unusual repose of the man; nothing seems to ruffle him. He is gradually
acquiring a kind of benignity. He is pronouncedly less "tense" than
Chiang Kai-shek.

We talked about Roosevelt's foreign policy, differences between the
Democrats and Republicans, Chinese Industrial Cooperatives, new problems of
the United Front, the European war, relations between the Eighth Route Army
and the Kuomintang, and Soviet policy in Europe and its effects on China.
We read the day's news and discussed it.

Mao thought Roosevelt would get America into the war. It was (in
Europe) a "pure imperialist war." Before Chamberlain dragged England into it
without the U.S.S.R. it might have been a "progressive war" but now it was
purely imperialistic, Mao thought. Communists in the United States had
supported Roosevelt in the past but they would not now support him if he
entered the war.

Mao was somewhat puzzled by the attitudes of the two American parties
toward the war. He thought it curious that during the last war (World War I)
the Democrats in power had taken the country into it with Republican support.
In this war the Democrats again were in power and Roosevelt was calling for
a change in the neutrality policy of the United States and wished to lead the

---

*These interviews were transcribed and published in full in the China Weekly
Review (Jan. 13 and 20, 1940). See also, The Battle for Asia (New York,
1941), 280-302.

nation into the war, but Republicans were still strongly isolationist.
Why should that be? Didn't the Republicans represent big finance capital?
They could make the most money out of war.

I questioned such a schematic division of the two parties, as capitalists of different kinds were to be found in both parties, the "big finance
capitalists" always retaining a hand in both. Foreign policy reflected
pressures in domestic policy, and a change in public opinion, including
labor opinion, could bring about a revised stand by the Republicans. I
cited the change in attitude toward abrogation of the commercial treaty
with Japan as an example.

Mao pointed out "contradictions" in United States policy, i.e., despite
(moves toward?) the abrogation of the Japanese treaty, American merchants
continued to sell raw materials to Japan, more now than ever before.

Acknowledging this, I said it was no more curious than Britain's
policy of arming and financing Hitler, even turning over the reserves
of the Czeck Bank to him and selling him everything he wanted, right to
the outbreak of the war. Also consider the U.S.S.R. policy toward Japan.
Russia was selling oil to Japan from Sakhalin and maintaining trade, and
had renewed Japanese fishing rights in Soviet waters. When Japanese fish
were purchased in England a terrific howl arose from the Left, but not a
word was said against Russia for selling Japan the fishing concession.

Mao laughed and said that Stalin had learned that from Roosevelt.
Throughout our conversation he frequently used the word Stalin as a synonym
for the U.S.S.R.

Russia was still selling arms and supplies to Germany, yet maintaining a nominally "neutral" position (I said). Tomorrow Russia might be at
war with Germany. I said that in that case "contradictions" between
capitalism and socialism would become so confused--"like a ball of yarn
entangled by a cat and becoming more and more entangled as one attempts
to straighten it out"--that no one could foresee the outcome. Was that
not so? (I asked).

Mao said Stalin did not have to worry about a German attack now. "Hitler
is in Stalin's pocket." He said this half humorously and I asked if he
really meant it. He replied that he meant it _shih-fen chih wu_--fifty per
cent.

In answer to other questions Mao indicated that he was convinced that
Stalin had made his pact with Hitler in order to forestall Chamberlain from
building a coalition against Russia. Chamberlain had told Hitler he must
attack Russia or England would fight (he said). If he had fought Russia,
Chamberlain was prepared to give Hitler Poland, Rumania, Yugoslavia and the
Baltic states. Stalin had made a counter-offer which was more attractive
than Chamberlain's.

(This appeared to be said figuratively; Mao seemed to enjoy the thought
that Stalin had played a smart trick on the despised umbrella man—who was
then being lampooned in cartoons and clay puppet figurines in Yenan.)

Mao asked me for news of industrial cooperatives—how they had begun
and so on.

I explained Chinese Industrial Cooperatives from the earliest days in
Shanghai, through the formation of the International Committee, down to
fund-raising committees abroad. I stressed its value to guerrillas. Mao
lay back and puffed his cigarette, looking through slits in his eyes while
I made this (rather overlong) speech. He then said he fully supported
Indusco and had done so ever since I wrote to him from Hankow describing the
movement. He made this statement:

"We support the idea of building many small industries as an important
part of economic reconstruction during the war. Even if Chinese Industrial
Cooperatives can do nothing for front-line areas and the guerrilla districts
behind enemy lines, the work they are doing is very important in helping to
restore industry in the rear. But it is in the war areas and the guerrilla
districts in the enemy's rear that industrial cooperatives are most needed
and will find the warmest welcome from our troops, from the people, and
from the government. By this means we can help achieve manifold objectives:
(1) stop the penetration of enemy goods from the occupied cities to rural
bases of guerrilla warfare; (2) utilize China's raw materials and resources
for our own industries and prevent Japan from exploiting them; (3) create
economically self-sufficient bases of guerrilla war to support protracted
struggle; (4) train our unemployed and unskilled labor so that Japan cannot
utilize it against us; (5) maintain village prosperity by giving the farmers
needed manufactures in exchange for food. All friends of China should
support this progressive movement.

"Chinese Industrial Cooperatives ought to devote first attention to the needs of guerrilla areas. The struggle against Japanese imperialism in the occupied areas is of first importance, for if Japan succeeds in conquering (consolidating) those areas there can hardly be a future for cooperative industry any more than for any other kind of industry."

Mao agreed to write out this statement for circulation among overseas Chinese. He later did so—elaborating quite a lot and adding some patriotic flourishes. The letter was released to overseas Chinese through the International Committee of the C.I.C. at Hongkong and helped to raise funds.

I was in Yenan for ten days or so during this visit and saw Mao several times on purely social occasions, dropping in to have tea with him or to play poker. He had also learned to play bridge; I sat in a game with him and his wife until one in the morning. We alternated bridge and poker several nights in a row. I have forgotten whether it was Ma Hai-teh who taught him these games, or one of my own "students" from my 1936 days in Pao-an. In my diary I noted that Mao was a big gambler at poker and a poor bluffer, but an entertaining player. He took the whole thing too lightly to be agreeable to any serious poker player; he enjoyed himself. The stakes were large but entirely fictitious.

Mao's health has improved; he is gaining weight. I asked him whether he preferred military life or the kind of administrative or sedentary life he was then leading. He said military life was much to be preferred; his bowels had worked better during the battle of Changsha than at any other time . . . .

In casual conversation Mao asked a number of questions about American geography, climate and people. He asked whether the Negroes had gained any new voting power in the South and what were the statistics on illiteracy. He asked about the American Indians and how they were treated. He was surprised to learn that no Catholic had ever been elected president of the United States. Was there a strong religious conflict in America? How did most people get married there? He had read about Yellowstone National Park and asked if I had seen it. He thought China should have a park like that . . . . He said he had never been able to understand how prohibition laws could have been passed in America. He seemed greatly interested in every scientific and mechanical aspect of American civilization, as well as being strongly attracted to California by all he had heard of it. He had wanted to travel abroad but felt that he could never do so until he had seen more of China. Although he had walked across a great deal of it, China still held many wonders he had yet to see. China was, like Soviet Russia, "a world in itself."

> By this time Mao had married a motion picture actress who had come to Yenan after the outbreak of the Sino-Japanese war in 1937. Early in that year Mao had quarreled with his wife, Ho Chih-chen 賀志珍 , who had made the Long March from Kiangsi with him to Pao-an, where I saw them together in 1936, and they had been divorced. Mrs. Mao later had gone to Russia with their small son. Mao remarried the following year.

2. Mao Tse-tung and Chang Kuo-t'ao 張國燾

Elsewhere in these pages I have quoted Po Ku on the Communist party's theoretical and practical position concerning the "hegemony" of the Chinese revolution during the United Front against Japan. I have also reported what I was told about Mao Tse-tung's frigid reception of Heinz Shippe ("Asiaticus") when in 1938 he arrived in Yenan expecting to be praised for his critique of Red Star Over China on grounds that I had erroneously asserted that the Chinese Communists had not abandoned either their claims to leadership over the workers and peasants or their pretensions to ultimate leadership of the national (bourgeois-democratic) revolution.*

On my return to Yenan in 1939 Mao made no direct reference to Shippe's visit but he said, when I asked about it, that Red Star Over China (which he had read in full translation) had correctly reported party policies and his own views. At a mass meeting of party and military personnel in Yenan he also took the trouble to introduce me, personally, as the author of a "truthful book about us," without qualifications. Perhaps he meant that as an answer not only to Shippe but to American Communists who had also disputed parts of Red Star which dealt with theory and pointed out past errors of the Comintern in China. The book was actually banned from Communist party bookshops in the United States during one period.

On reflection it also occurred to me that Shippe's arguments may well have struck Mao as being repetitive of the line earlier advanced by Chang Kuo-t'ao, which the Politburo rejected as "right opportunism" and

---

*See Pacific Affairs (June 1938).

"liquidationism." As students of the period may recall, Chang had dramati-
cally opposed Mao and the rest of the Politburo at Maoerhkai in August 1935,
when fundamental questions of "hegemony" during a (then) hypothetical
Kuomintang-Communist united front against Japan were debated. Chang at
that time disobeyed the party's orders--for reasons which, in 1938, he
explained as follows:

> "I still remember my argument with Mao (Tse-tung) in 1935 when the
> First (Front) Army, led by Mao, and the Fourth (Front) Army, led by
> myself, met in western Szechwan. At that time Mao regarded the Long
> March as a success. He insisted on a Central Soviet Socialist Republic.
> I opposed this (plan). I considered the Long March a failure and I
> proposed a fundamental compromise with the Central (Kuomintang)
> government . . . . "*

Chang wished to stay in Sikang or move to western Kansu (he said),
abandoning the soviet bases and independent power, apparently with the hope
of making a good bargain with Chiang Kai-shek offering himself and his
officers a respectable place in the "national" army in a thoroughgoing
integration with the Kuomintang. But Mao demanded adherence to the Politburo
decision to create a united anti-Japanese front based on political (i.e.,
party) and military co-existence. He insisted on moving into Shensi to
combine with and expand the soviets and partisan forces there as part of
a dual policy which also called for cessation of civil war and appeals for
the formation of a national defense government--Mao hoping that Japanese
pressure would meanwhile intensify and compel even important Kuomintang
generals to negotiate with the Reds as peers.

The duel between Chang and Mao on the high plateaus near Tibet was
probably the most critical moment in the history of Mao's rise to supremacy.
Mao had long before this established himself as the top political leader who
(at least in South China) commanded the confidence of the Red Army, princi-
pally through the unshakeable loyalty of Chu Teh. This factor has perhaps
been underestimated in some analyses of Mao's position during the Kiangsi
days, when the matter of military power or real control of what the Reds
called "living forces" was at all times more decisive than the seeming

---

* See "Chang Kuo-t'ao's Appeal to Countrymen," issued in Hankow, May 2, 1938.
I quote from a rough translation made at the time: the Chinese original is
in my files.

weight of one or another political argument or "line" or combination against
Mao in the struggle within the Politburo. Over the theoretical debates
there always hung the fact and the record of Mao's inseparability from
Chu Teh. This was the insurmountable obstacle for all Mao's rivals in the
South—his influence first of all with Chu Teh, but also with P'eng Teh-huai,
Lo P'ing-hui 羅炳輝 , Liu Po-ch'eng 劉伯承 , Lin Piao, Hsiao K'e
and Ho Lung.

In Moukung-hsien, Szechwan, in June 1935, Mao Tse-tung met an aspirant
to supreme leadership, Chang Kuo-t'ao, who appeared capable of challenging
Mao's popularity with the army. He was not only Mao's peer as a founding
member of the party and a comrade of demonstrated competence in internal
organizational struggle, but was then chief political commissar of armed
forces—the Fourth Front Red Army—which somewhat outnumbered Red survivors
who had come up from Kiangsi with Mao.

Mao still carried his title, as "Chairman of the All-China Soviet
Government," and was superior to Chang Kuo-t'ao, as vice-chairman of the
same; but Chang was also chairman of the Szechwan regional soviet area, then
the largest under Communist power. At the Tsunyi (Kweichow) Conference
Mao's all-China leadership had again been affirmed by the Politburo, with
the support of the Central Committee; but Chang's followers had not been
fully represented, and the decisions had to be re-debated, for which the
Maoerhkai Conference was held in Szechwan. There the general line advocated
by Mao Tse-tung was confirmed, as was the strategy of concentration of
forces in the Northwest, against the opposition of Chang Kuo-t'ao, who
wished to remain and build the chief Red base in the Sikang-Szechwan plateau.

After being voted down in the Maoerhkai Conference, however, Chang
appeared to accept the decision to proceed northward. He placed the Fourth
Front Army under the command of Chu Teh, who also led the much smaller
Fourth and Ninth Red Army Corps (his chief of staff being Liu Po-ch'eng)
to form the western column of the projected march to Shensi. In Maoerhkai
Mao Tse-tung remained with the balance of the First Front Army under P'eng
Teh-huai, to constitute the eastern column of the march. After Chu Teh's
forces and the Fourth Front Red Army separated from the others and moved
northwestward, they ran into heavy rains and a flood which made one of the
principal rivers of the region impassable. Chang Kuo-t'ao then wished to

turn back into the Sungpan and abandon the advance. Chu Teh insisted on
returning eastward to Maoerhkai and following Mao's column. While they were
arguing about this some enemy troops blocked their route to Maoerhkai. This
much I learned from Mao Tse-tung and others.* A recent biography of Chu Teh
takes up the story from there as follows:

> "That same night (of the flood) Chang Kuo-tao brought up special
> troops of the Fourth Front Red Army, surrounded General Headquarters, and
> took Chu Teh and his staff prisoner. Chang ordered Chu Teh to obey two
> commands:
> "The first was that he denounce Mao Tse-tung and cut off all relations
> with him.
> "General Chu replied: 'You can no more cut me off from Mao than you
> can cut a man in half.'
> "Chang's second command was that Chu denounce the party decision to
> move into north China and behind the anti-Japanese, anti-Chiang war of
> liberation. General Chu replied:
> "'I helped make that decision. I cannot oppose it.'
> "Chang Kuo-tao said he would give Chu Teh time to think things over,
> and if he still refused to obey these two orders, he would be shot.
> Chu Teh replied: 'That is within your power. I cannot prevent you.
> I will not obey your orders!'
> "A number of factors prevented Chang Kuo-tao from carrying out
> his threat. First, there were the Ninth and Fifth Red Army Corps, who
> wanted to take Chu Teh and his staff back to the eastern column. Chang
> Kuo-tao wanted them not to try! Faced with this situation, which would
> have led to bloody fighting on the high plateaus of central Asia, Chu
> Teh and his staff finally turned back with Chang Kuo-tao."**

At this time and throughout the following winter Chu Teh's loyalty to
Mao probably decided not only the fate of Chang Kuo-t'ao but averted what
might have been a disastrous split in the Red forces. Struggling toward
the Northwest with his small band of exhausted troops Mao was left in doubt
concerning the true nature of events in his rear—doubts not to be finally
resolved for nearly a year. All depended on Chu, for whatever relative
attractions Mao and Chang had for the party hierarchy and bureaucracy it
was obvious that neither could prevail without the support of the top combat
Communists.

Chu Teh was not only a popular commander-in-chief among all the Red
officers but he already amounted to a kind of living legend among the rank

---

*See <u>Red Star Over China</u>, 191-92.
**Agnes Smedley, <u>The Great Road</u> (New York, 1936), 331.

and file. In Szechwan especially, his native province, his name alone was
enough to win and hold a following. Many of the officers and men of the
Fourth Front Red Army were Chu's fellow provincials, and he could speak to
them in their own dialect. Chang Kuo-t'ao had a coterie of staff officers
personally loyal to him, but Chu Teh was superior officer over all of them,
including, of course, Hsü Hsiang-ch'ien 徐向前 , military commander of
the Fourth Front Red Army. Chang's relationship with Hsü Hsiang-ch'ien
was close, but not as close as the Chu-Mao unity. After all, Hsü could not
oppose Chu Teh without being guilty of both military and political insubordi-
nation, and Hsü, an intellectual, was also a good soldier--a Whampoa
officer, a classmate of Lin Piao, and a student of Chou En-lai--and had a
record of loyalty to party decisions dating back to the Canton Commune.

There was also the fact that Liu Po-ch'eng, Chu's chief of staff,
was a Szechwanese and his two corps might have had to be destroyed if
Chu Teh were harmed. These factors, plus the knowledge that the Second
Front Army (under Generals Ho Lung and Hsiao K'e) was on its way up from
Hunan to Szechwan, must have been enough to cause Chang not to demand any
more of Chu Teh and his men during the months that followed than their
support in his attempt to carry out his own "line" aimed at building a
powerful base in Sikang.

Meanwhile Mao's column advanced into the Northwest and, after recuperat-
ing, scored important successes in Kansu, Ninghsia and Shensi. Joined by
Liu Chih-tan's 劉志丹 and Hsu Hai-tung's 徐海東 forces, the First
Front Red Army was able to invade Shansi province, where local forces proved
easy prey to the Reds' new "fight-and-persuade" or "talk-and-fight" tactics.
Chang's base in the far west, on the other hand, gradually became an unten-
able cul-de-sac. Large and powerful provincial and Central government forces
were mobilized against it and recruitment and procurement became extremely
difficult. With the arrival of the Second Front Red Army a military
conference was held and this time Chang accepted the joint demand of Chu Teh,
Ho Lung, Hsiao K'e, Lo P'ing-hui and Liu Po-ch'eng that all their forces
move northward, to avoid encirclement and annihilation.

Chang's behavior would doubtless have finished his career in any case, but with the de facto alliance that Mao and Chou En-lai had by 1936 brought about between the Red Army and Chang Hsüeh-liang's Manchurian troops in Shensi, Mao's judgment seemed manifestly vindicated by all events. It is interesting to note, however, that despite Chang's violation of Politburo orders--at heavy costs in time, lives and opportunities--no severe action was demanded against him by Mao. He was not formally "tried" for his offenses until early 1937. He was then removed from command and ordered to undergo a period of "self-criticism and study of his errors." As nearly as I could learn when I visited Yenan in 1939 no serious precautions had been taken to prevent his departure from that area in April 1938. Apparently he had not been denied freedom of movement within a restricted area, and he was permitted visitors. It was, in fact, some Kuomintang officers whom he met while they were on a formal visit to Yenan whom he followed out of his own world, to Sian.

In Chang Kuo-t'ao's "Appeal," issued soon after he reached the Generalissimo's headquarters (Hankow, May 1938), he made no reference to any attempt to prevent him from leaving Yenan. He had originally meant to go only to Sian, but on reaching there (he reported) he became so impressed with Kuomintang military and economic planning that he decided to "go on to Hankow, intending to discuss with leaders of the Central Organization of the Chinese Communist Party . . . the best possible ways of resistance and reconstruction."*

Chang may have had in mind speaking to Chou En-lai, Po Ku and Wang Ming, who were all in Hankow at the time, but following his arrival he discovered that he was "then declared dismissed from the party." So his "Appeal" stated. Evidently he had not been dropped from the party rolls even after he left Yenan for Sian, but only when he openly joined the Kuomintang camp. Apparently neither party members nor army personnel accompanied Chang, and there does not seem to be any reliable evidence that "large numbers of his followers" were "captured and executed," as has lately been suggested in some quarters.** Hsü Hsiang-ch'ien was succeeded in

---

*"Chang Kuo-t'ao's Appeal to Countrymen."
**E.g., Robert North, Moscow and Chinese Communists (Stanford, 1953), 180.

command of his troops by Liu Po-ch'eng in the middle of 1937, but he was
still around Yenan as a staff officer and was interviewed by foreigners.*
It may be remembered that the "new democracy" was in full swing in 1938, and
many Kuomintang members were going back and forth and even participating in
some activities in the Communist-held areas, while both foreign and Chinese
non-Communist travelers moved about fairly freely then. It is hardly cred-
ible that any large-scale purge could have occurred without being detected
and reported, or at least being rumored, at the time.

Such facts and conditions may be borne in mind when one is confronted
by the recent tendency to present Chang as a purge victim--in the sense that
he represented an important point of view or minority with which Mao could
contend only by violent suppression. What seems true now, as it did in 1938,
is that Chang's own miscalculations, abetted by the caprices of history, had
by then denied him any future party role of significance. It is my own
recollection that at the time he was in Hankow sophisticated Kuomintang
leaders as well as Communists regarded Chang simply as a self-exiled apostate.
It is perhaps notable that even Ch'en Li-fu 陳立夫 , for whom he
worked, did not attempt to exploit Chang as a "purgee," while Chang's own
"Appeal," written at that time, in no way supported that contention.

Lo Fu wrote:** "In his 'Appeal' Chang (Kuo-t'ao) also asserted that
he had (finally) gone north (from Szechwan) as a result of his determination to support the decision adopted by the Communist International concerning the anti-Japanese United Front in December, 1935. That is laughable.
His move to the north did not really come about as his 'Appeal' claims but
was simply the result of victory for the party's line, and of pressure from
comrades in the Second and Fourth armies.

"Facts also proved that it was not the Central (Party) Organization,
but Chang himself, who confessed with tears that he was to be blamed. Now I
present to my readers the following paragraph selected from 'My Faults,'
written by Chang himself on April 6, 1937:

---

*Nym Wales, Inside Red China, 132-41.
**"Comments on 'Chang Kuo-t'ao's Appeal to Countrymen,'" by Lo Fu. Quoted from
a rather poor translation in my possession acquired in Hankow, 1938. The
original place and date of publication are not stated; probably it appeared
in the party press at Yenan.

'Those comrades who revealed my faults clearly during the Enlarged Congress of the Central Political Bureau have made me understand them even more. Certainly my errors have originated from my whole political line and display my "retreatism" based on my right-inclined opportunism. These faults not only had bad results but also injured the revolution considerably, and indirectly aided the anti-revolutionary forces.'-- Activities of the Party, vol. 31 (Apr. 12, 1937); published by the Central Organization of the Chinese Communist Party.

"We believe that Chang's comprehension of the anti-Japanese United Front differs from that of the Central Organization of the C.C.P. Far away in Sikang and Tibet Chang adhered to the position of a 'T'u-shih' when the party was struggling to form an anti-Japanese United Front. Informed of the new policy, Chang simply laughed at the idea without believing in the possibility at all. But once the United Front became a reality he then turned to the other extreme and proposed the abolition of the C.C.P."

Chang's own "Appeal" actually called upon the Yenarites to accept (1) the San Min Chu I, "without any reservations of any kind, not to say prejudices, arguments and propaganda which are contradictory to those principles"; (2) "nationalization" of the Eighth Route Army and the border governments; and (3) "unification of one more step" including abandonment of the land revolution, absolute obedience to the Central Government, and recognition that "the Kuomintang (is) the most revolutionary party and Mr. Chiang (Kai-shek) the only leader."*

In answer to a question from me during my last interviews with Mao Tse-tung in 1939, concerning this matter of leadership in the United Front period, Mao was so unequivocal that it is difficult to see how the myth of the Communists being "mere agrarian reformers" could ever have survived.

"Many people," I said, "now assert that the Chinese Communists are in fact no longer social revolutionaries, but mere reformists. How do you answer them? Do you still maintain that the Chinese revolution is (I quoted him) 'anti-imperialist and anti-feudal, with the possibility of transformation, at a certain state, into socialist revolution' and that the responsibility of the Communist Party is to lead the nation toward that revolution?"

---

* "Chang Kuo-t'ao's Appeal to Countrymen"; underlining mine.

"We are always revolutionaries," Mao replied, "and we are never reformists. There are two main objectives in the thesis of the Chinese revolution. The first consists of the realization of the tasks of a national democratic revolution. The other is social revolution. The latter must be achieved, and completely achieved. For the present the revolution is national and democratic in character, but after a certain stage it will be transformed into social revolution . . . unless our work in the present phase is a failure, in which case there is no early possibility of social revolution."*

---

* China Weekly Review (Jan. 13, 1940).

XII. LO FU 洛甫 ON PARTY QUESTIONS

1. On Trotskyism

The following data were supplied to me by Lo Fu at Pao-an during a long interview on July 19, 1936, or in brief sessions later. Lo Fu was at this time secretary of the Chinese Communist Party Central Committee, a position which he had held since 1934, in Kiangsi. Lo Fu gave me an autobiography which I could not, owing to space limitations, include in Red Star Over China. Later it appeared in Nym Wales' Inside Red China.

The statements below were elicited by questions from me of which I possess no record, but they are easily to be inferred from the text.

Lo Fu, who lived in America for a year or so and took some courses at the University of California, spoke in English and without anyone else present. He said:

"The Trotskyists do not understand the real character of the Chinese revolution.

"They believe that all tasks of the revolution already lie in the hands of the proletariat; they think that it is a time for the struggle for power against the bourgeoisie. We believe that we are in a struggle against semi-feudal and semi-colonial society, and therefore it is in character a bourgeois-democratic revolution. The main task of the revolution must be shared by the proletariat, the petty-bourgeoisie, and the vast masses of the peasantry.

"Trotsky ignores the role of the peasantry in the Chinese revolution just as he ignored it in the Russian revolution of 1905 and up to 1917. From our standpoint the proletariat will play a role of hegemony over the petty-bourgeoisie and the peasantry in the Chinese revolution. To the Trotskyists the role of hegemony of the Chinese proletariat does not exist, because they see it only as the class of dictatorship, not as part of a coalition of forces.

"Is it possible for the Chinese proletariat to play this leading role (hegemony) in the revolution? We certainly recognize that Chinese capitalism is backward; nevertheless it has a big role in Chinese economy. The number of workers in the imperialist and native capitalist industries is now about three million. This is not a small beginning. Secondly, because of the intensity of capitalist oppression, because of the key nature of such

industries in Chinese economy as a whole, the workers are destined to play a
role of very great importance . . . . While the numbers of workers may not
be very great in proportion to the population, their strength and importance
are fully understood by the Communist party and therefore they can be utilized
to the fullest extent.

"Thirdly, China is fortunate in having a revolutionary party which has
had clear aims and uncluttered vision from an early date. The British
workers, for example, are more numerous, but they have been misled and
dominated by the Labour party, which works in the interest of (preserving)
the bourgeoisie. China has no Labour party--the special gift of imperialism
(to its proletariat), the gift of surplus value. The Chinese workers have
from the beginning been under the leadership of the Communist party, and thus
it depends very much on the character of that leadership alone whether China
is to have a successful revolution. Under Communist leadership the Chinese
proletariat has played a very active role, beginning with its training
(experience) during strikes against imperialism in Hankow, in Canton,
Shanghai, etc. And now in the rural districts the proletariat also is a
leading part of the Red Army. The army as a whole is proletarian in its
aims just because it _is_ under the leadership of the Communist party and no
other party can seize the leadership.

"Thus the Red Army is not an army of the peasantry, although its troops
are largely drawn from the peasantry. _It is an army of the Communist party,_
first of all, which is a party with clear proletarian discipline, a clear
proletarian program, and a clear strategy and purpose such as no peasant
rebellions of the past have ever had. Peasant rebellion merely changes one
group of feudalists for another. The Taiping Rebellion had that weakness,
for example.

"Why do we not enter the cities (if we represent the proletariat)?
This is not because the proletariat is so backward. It is because imperialism and native reaction concentrate their main strength there. If it were
not for the help of foreign imperialism we could enter and take the cities.
If Chiang could not get foreign guns and airplanes--the equipment and
techniques of imperialism--we would seize the strategic cities easily.
Because of the uneven development of capitalist imperialism in China, however,

we are able to gather strength in areas less dominated by imperialism, to gain experience there, and to prepare for the final realization of our aims. Our development is thus quite different from that of the Russian revolution. There the whole country fell at once into the hands of the revolution once the Tsarist regime was destroyed. Here in China we must first seize the whole country and then the Nanking regime will collapse.

"Why land distribution? Because we consider that the main task of the Chinese revolution is the task of the agrarian anti-imperialist revolution. Without the help of the peasantry it is impossible for the revolution to succeed."

> Trotskyist literature of the period condemned land division as characteristic of a peasant rebellion or agrarian reform movement. Based on the backward elements of the peasantry (Trotskyists contended) the Red Army could rise no higher than its source. It could not transform the revolution into a true proletarian revolution.

"In the Russian revolution, the Red Army was formed <u>after</u> the revolution began, to consolidate the Communists' seizure of power. In the Chinese revolution, the Red Army has to form and develop as the revolution itself forms and develops, <u>before</u> the seizure of (all state) power.

"Trotskyists maintain on the one hand that the peasantry is backward, reactionary, non-revolutionary; on the other hand they say that the proletariat in China is too small, too weak, too backward, too demoralized to lead the revolution. Therefore their synthesis ends in the <u>thesis</u> of the bourgeois revolution led <u>by</u> the bourgeoisie and the imperialists."

> Trotskyists at one point held that continued Communist party struggle for power in the face of the fascist menace was threatening all the democratic gains of the working class everywhere in China; the Red Army was held to be "objectively" helping Japan.

"<u>The Communist Party has no intention, however, of waiting for imperialism, under the guise of native capitalist leadership, to consolidate control over the country</u>.* All the nationalities in Turkestan, the Mongols in Outer Mongolia, had little or no industrial proletariat. Still today they are building socialism. Why? The validity of the revolution depends upon the proletarian leadership as represented by the Communist party--in this case the Communist Party of the Soviet Union.

---

* Underlining mine.

"Development of revolution in any single country does not depend solely on numbers of its proletariat. It depends to a great extent on the leadership given it by the world proletarian party--the Comintern--and the determination of correct tactics and strategy by the Communist party. Chinese Communists, the leaders of the proletariat, draw upon the collective experience of the world proletariat for tactics and success. It must be remembered that in China the party also draws upon a large section of the petty-bourgeoisie, already proletarianized (economically and intellectually), for its guidance and leadership.

"What are the conditions for a successful seizure of the big cities by the revolution? In its pure form the best guarantee of success is an offensive by the Red Army from without, combined with a proletarian-led insurrection from within. There may or may not be also 'White' army insurrections, national revolutionary movements, general strikes, disintegration of the defending White forces, or defection of important sections of the national bourgeois armies to the side of revolution."

2. Stages of the Revolution

1919-25. Period of Preparation (May 4 to May 30, 1925)
1925-27. Period of the Great Revolution (vs. imperialism-feudalism)
1927.   Canton Commune
1927-31. First Soviet Revolution, with emphasis on agrarian revolution
1931-   (The anti-Japanese) National Liberation Movement, in which the Red Army will play a leading and decisive role.

"The essential difference between past and present is the modification of Red Army and Soviet policy to fit into the need for national liberation as the precondition of class liberation. (1925-27: thesis; 1927-31: anti-thesis; 1931-: synthesis.)

"Perhaps the Chinese revolution may not develop, after this period (war of liberation) in the same way as the Russian revolution. That is, our party may win leadership over the national revolution and thus be able to bring China through to socialism by peaceful means and by peaceful liquidation of the classes. The violence of the revolution may be expended in external struggle, in the war against imperialism. During this period imperialism must, therefore, be exploited as the basis for establishing national unity and the preconditions of socialist victory and policy."

3. Socialism and Foreign Enterprises

"All the important capitalist enterprises in China are now in the hands of foreign imperialism. It is impossible to conceive of success in building a free Chinese economy while this condition exists. However, the greatest immediate menace to Chinese economy as well as to China's political sovereignty is Japanese imperialism. We are concerned in this period* with eliminating Japanese imperialist interests, and therefore we advocate prompt confiscation of such interests and their operation to benefit the Chinese people in their struggle for national liberation. As for other foreign imperialism, we are ready to pursue a moderate course, purchasing vital interests according to Soviet law, with special consideration given to those powers which help or cooperate with us in our war against Japan."

4. Miscellaneous Questions

a. Party Training

"The first Communist schools were organized in Shanghai, but it was not until the Kiangsi soviets were set up that the first 'full course' in Marxism was offered--at the Marx Kung-ch'an Hsueh-hsiao in Chi-an (Kiangsi), in 1933. Its curriculum: (1) The ABC of Marxism-Leninism; (2) Principles of Party Construction and Party Work; (3) Soviet Construction: Principles of Soviet Organization, Trade Union and Peasant Union Organization, Mass Organization Formations, etc; (4) Lecture Courses: Problems of Agrarian and Industrial Economy (peasant and worker problems); Cultural Work (propaganda etc.); Partisan Organization and Training. Three to six months of full-time study were required of students taking these courses."

---

* Underlining mine.

b. Party Membership

"At present total membership in the Northwest soviet districts (including armed forces) is about 40,000, out of a total population of about 400,000. In Kiangsi and Fukien soviets, with 3,000,000 inhabitants, party membership was 150,000. In all the Yangtze Valley soviet areas (Kiangsi, Fukien, Honan, Kiangsu, Anhui, Hupeh, Hunan) total membership was formerly about 400,000. In North China today (1936) outside the Soviet areas, membership is about 10,000. At its highest period of prestige in Kiangsi, membership of the Chinese party may have been almost 400,000. Communist Youth membership was less than that."

c. Terror and Battle Statistics

Lo Fu says that the Communists imprisoned no more than 50,000 people for political reasons in their whole reign in the South. He estimates that more than 500,000 Communists have been killed since 1927. This includes 20,000 lost in the Canton Commune, about 10,000 killed in Shanghai in 1927, some 20,000 killed in Changsha, 1927-28, and about 20,000 killed in Wuhan in 1927. Formerly the Red Aid Society kept statistics on arrests and killings, but their members were also caught and killed, in the cities.

Apart from individual arrests and executions, some 3,000,000 people were killed to date in all five anti-Red campaigns, north and south of the Yangtze. In Kiangsi, the soviet district had a population of 2,500,000 when the republic was flourishing; after the last anti-Communist extermination campaign, when the Red Army was forced to flee, there were only 1,500,000 people left. In the Hupei-Honan-Anhui (E-yü-wan) soviet area, the population has decreased by 600,000 since the Kuomintang forces occupied it. Half a million people were killed in the "purge" of the Kiangsi-Hunan-Hupeh border district after the Kuomintang troops conquered there. In the north of Szechwan (where the Reds attacked and were severely attacked in turn) there was a population of about 1,000,000 (?). After the Red Army passed on the population was reduced by half. Red Army dead in the last campaign in Kiangsi were about 50,000.

Lo Fu insists that the Soviet government in the south "in all condemned and executed no more than 1,000 counter-revolutionaries" (i.e., political prisoners, apart from "class enemies"?). They executed four to five hundred landlords. Most landlords were ransomed and released; many were allowed to flee; many were absentees before the Red Army arrived. Several hundred usurers, fewer than 1,000 (says Lo Fu), were killed in Kiangsi. During the Long March fewer than 100 landlords and officials were executed; in all, not 100. Fewer than ten people--the worst usurers, landlords, corrupt officials--were killed in Shansi. Only two "spies" had been executed in Shansi.

d. Bolshevization of Conquered Territory

Lo Fu said: "When the Red Army takes a village it first calls a mass meeting of the whole population, explains the Red Army and its program. Then it calls for formation of a temporary village revolutionary committee by popular vote. The revolutionary committee then undertakes the first investigative duties preliminary to formation of a soviet. It gathers vital statistics on population, on land ownership and distribution, numbers of resident landlords, landowning peasants, rich peasants, middle peasants, poor and landless peasants, industrial workers, handicraft workers, merchants of various categories, etc. It gathers complaints against oppressors of the poor. The worst of these are then brought to trial before another mass meeting. The accused are brought forth and confronted by their denouncers. The meeting decides whether the offenses deserve punishment by death, hard labor, minor fines, or disfranchisement. Villagers are usually very fierce in their demands for death of the worst of the oppressors; the Red Army has to be a moderating influence. Afterward the villagers are more lenient in their attitude and ready to cooperate with the Red Army. As a rule they hate and despise usurers most of all. If the mass considers them guilty of extreme oppression they are killed."

e. Treatment of Prisoners

"Prisoners who are not too bad are put to work on state projects like
transportation or factory work (making uniforms) or copying books or printing,
etc. If they repent and show willingness to cooperate they are freed and
their right to vote and hold office is restored. Many are like this. Some
are freed without the right to vote.

"All the above was past practice in Kiangsi. Our present policy is to
free all political prisoners after detaining them for an educative period.
We kill nobody now . . . Yes, nobody, not even enemy officers. Formerly we
killed officers of the 'White' army of colonel or general rank, but not
others; now we free them after trying to win them over to the United Front.
The results of this are very good. Ordinary soldiers are freed, given $5.00
for transport charges (travel expenses) and released. Many stay with us and
join the Red Army. Even fascists are freed nowadays. Commanders receive
$30.00 to $50.00 for 'travel expenses.' One fascist commander was won over
by the Reds. If a big landlord is liked by the masses the Communists never
touch him—even in Kiangsi days we did not. We take his land and deprive
him of a vote and the right to join the Red Army. The Reds never exceed the
(spontaneous) demand of the masses.

"In Pao-an we have only one jail and it is a yao-fang of one room, like
any other.* If a crime is serious the prisoner is sent directly to the place
where he committed it, and the soviet decides what punishment he deserves.
Bandits, min-t'uan (militia) and enemy soldiers are treated alike. We try to
persuade them to accept Red law and help in anti-Japanese campaign (sic). If
their attitude is not bad they are freed, whether they are sympathetic or not.

"Ordinary criminals are detained a few days and criticized. Usually
the prisoner confesses his error and agrees to correct his conduct. Political
prisoners far outnumber others. The old feudal quarrels (family quarrels)
end under the soviet. Why did they fight each other before? Because the
landlords of one family would utilize their peasants to fight against those
of another. With the power of the landlords liquidated and land redistributed,
the peasants find they have no reason to quarrel with each other. They
work together, to learn and to build."

---

*I saw this jail later. There was one youth in it (guarded by one soldier)
who was allegedly a spy.

XIII. CH'EN KENG'S 陳賡 STORY

1. The Great Revolution

Ch'en Keng, commander of the First Division of the First Red Army Corps, was born in 1904 in Hsiang-hsien, Hunan, where so many other Reds were produced. His parents were landlords and he was given an early education in the classics, but at the age of thirteen he ran away from home to join the army. He had been affected by the May Fourth Movement and wanted to help save the country. His grandfather was a general in the Ch'ing dynasty and made a record for himself in command of Shanhaikuan. Ch'en regarded him as a hero when he was a youth.

He first joined the army of Lu Ti-p'ing 魯滌平 where P'eng Teh-huai also served. In 1922 his regimental commander, defeated by Wu P'ei-fu 吳佩孚 in militarists' warfare, became disgusted and decided to take a job as a director of the Hankow-Canton Railway. He offered Ch'en a minor post with him; having no choice at the time, Ch'en took it. Soon afterward the great strike at Wuhan affected the railway and Ch'en sympathized with the workers. He joined the Socialist Youth and worked as a courier and propagandist. In Canton he decided to leave the railway and resume his military career, when he had a chance to enter a school called Chiang Wu T'ang, under General Ch'eng Ch'ien 程潛 . Here he felt himself very repressed; he was denied all outside contacts. He therefore deserted the school and entered the first class at Whampoa Academy, where he was graduated as a lieutenant.

Ch'en's first action as a Whampoa officer was in the war against Ch'en Chiung-ming 陳炯明 , when he served under General T'ang Sheng-chih 唐生智 . He remained with General T'ang's army in the first phase of the Northern Expedition. He had meanwhile joined the Communist party, when cadets at Whampoa were given the alternative of adhering to the Kuomintang or the Communists.

In Wuhan, after the counter-revolution, Ch'en left his command and went to Nanch'ang, where he participated in the Red uprising of 1927. He next moved south with a detachment that took Juichin, Kiangsi; after the defeat he fled to Swatow, where an attempted Communist insurrection had been

defeated. He had been wounded in his right leg and had to be half-carried
by two bodyguards who loyally stayed with him. He was afraid to get treatment anywhere except in the Po-ai, a Japanese hospital in Swatow. While
he was convalescing there White troops hunting for Reds entered the hospital,
but a nurse named Li helped him to escape to a worker's room. The Japanese
superintendent dismissed the worker; then the gendarmes came for him
again. Again Miss Li saved him by hiding him in the latrine. After this
she and his bodyguards carried him to a steamer and got him aboard, staying
with him. When soldiers came on the steamer they arrested many fleeing
Reds, but Miss Li protected him once more by stating that he was a danger-
ously ill patient from her hospital whom she was taking to Hongkong.

The ship then departed for Hongkong, the first to reach there from
Swatow since the insurrection. The captain hoisted a distress flag and
British police came aboard, to arrest many wounded soldiers. Ch'en's
bodyguards put him on a piece of hospital linen used as a stretcher and he
spoke to the inspector in broken English, insisting that he was not a Red
but a telegraph operator from Chaochow. The Reds, he said, had attacked
his office and injured him; as there was no hospital in Chaochow he had
gone to the Japanese Po-ai (Fraternity) hospital in Swatow. The inspector
accepted his story and gave him an escort to a hotel in Hongkong. But
everybody came around to stare at "the Red from Swatow," and he fled from
that place.

His bodyguards carried him along the sidewalks but could not find
any place to stay, and once more he hid in a latrine.

Ch'en still had some money. He decided to buy a ticket on a steamer
to Shanghai. His bodyguards got him aboard, but just as the ship's bell
was ringing for departure time the purser became suspicious and put him
ashore. Then a sailor spoke to him and asked him if he really was a "Red
from Swatow." Being desperate and near suicide, he decided to throw himself
on the man's mercy and tell the truth. The sailor then helped to get him
back on the ship and hid him among some bananas and oranges, where he slept
till they reached Swatow.

When Ch'en came out of hiding again he saw a youth carrying a mattress
and being led to a place near him by the same friendly sailor. Ch'en

recognized him as a Red divisional commander named Chou; he had evidently
been helped aboard the ship at Swatow. Ch'en covered his face with a newspaper and all at once began to read: "These Swatow newspapers are right up
to the minute. It says here that a Red divisional commander named Chou
will be on board this ship." They greeted each other joyously and stayed
together after they reached Shanghai, where the two bodyguards also accompanied them to the same hotel, acting as servants. Here the party got
Ch'en into Niu's hospital, where his leg finally healed. Comrade Chou
later went to join Ho Lung's army and was killed in battle.

At Niu's hospital Ch'en found a number of Whampoa students, one of
whom recognized him and asked how he hurt his knee. All the Whampoa
cadets soon knew about it. Their Shanghai leader came to see them and also
called on Ch'en; he did not believe his story and called Ch'en a liar. Ch'en fled
from the hospital; he was about well, anyway. One day soon afterward Dr. Niu
recognized him on the street. He stopped his car, jumped out, and shook
hands with him. "If you had told us you were a Red," he said, "we would have
put you in a better room!" Later they became good friends.

2. Arrests and Escapes

Ch'en did party work in Shanghai for two years and then was sent to
join Hsü Hsiang-ch'ien's Fourth Army in Anhui. He assumed command of the
Twelfth Division. During the Fourth Extermination Campaign he was again
wounded, this time in his left leg. After recovering he rejoined the division and fought through Anhui and Hupeh to Honan. Then (in 1933) he was sent
to "locate the party" in Shensi, in anticipation of possible moves there.
He missed his contacts in south Shensi and was soon taken prisoner by the
local militia. He convinced them he was a businessman and was released. He
was arrested again and escaped. A few days later he was sleeping in a farmhouse when min-t'uan discovered him and carried him to a small village. That
night he gave his guards some money for opium and wine. When they fell
asleep he moved the table away from the door and got away. He was now
completely "lost" and too far from the Red Army to re-establish contact.
He walked on to the Lunghai railway and went to Shanghai to get new directives.

In Shanghai Ch'en learned that the Fourth Front Army (under Hsü
Hsiang-ch'ien and Chang Kuo-t'ao) had already reached Szechwan. He was
ordered to join Hsü Hai-tung's Fifteenth Army Corps, which was then
moving into Honan and south Shensi. His leg needed further attention and
he again went to Niu's hospital, where Dr. Niu quickly got him well. After
one month he was ready to leave, but the night before his departure he
went to see a movie. There he was recognized by a renegade party member,
Ku Shun-chang 顧順章 , who followed him out of the theater. On the
street Ku spoke to him, saying he was not a renegade and not to be afraid.
Ch'en knocked him down and started to run. Ku had a whistle which he blew.
Police surrounded Ch'en and he was caught and taken to the Ssu-ma-lu and
Avenue Road Jail. There he was imprisoned with Liao Ch'eng-chih 廖承志 ,
the son of Liao Chung-k'ai 廖仲凱 .

Ch'en was beaten by whips and then given electric shocks in attempts
to make him supply the names of Communists. He had bribed some guards to
get him cigarettes, which he swallowed, and this somewhat drugged or
poisoned him. The torture method was unsuccessful. Afterward he talked
to other prisoners and guards about the Red Army; even "Lampson," the
British agent, listened with interest and was kind to him. But despite
their changed, sympathetic attitude they got no names from him. He was
then moved from the International Settlement to the Chinese city, together
with Liao and Lo Teng-hsien 羅登賢 , a member of the Central Committee
who was later executed. When put in a car, they shouted slogans along
the road.

His history was well known, and Ch'en considered that he had no chance
to live. At the jail he was chained to an iron bar. A few days later
Ku Shun-chang, who had turned him in, arrived and tried to persuade him to
leave the Communists and join the Kuomintang. He said the revolution had
failed, Communist principles wouldn't work in China, and many Reds had now
taken advantage of the Generalissimo's generosity. "You will be pleased to
hear," he said, "that Mr. Chiang has sent many telegrams about you, asking
that you be given special treatment." Ch'en replied that Ku was a traitor
and that he was not like that. Ku later sent him fruits and presents, but
he scorned them.

3. Ch'en and Chiang Kai-shek

Nevertheless, Ch'en was soon transferred to Nanking, at Chiang Kai-shek's order. As his reputation for escaping was well known, he was chained to a girl comrade and put aboard a prison car with barred windows, under heavy guard. They both sang the "International" as the train stood at the station, and also on arrival at Nanking. There the commandant of the gendarmery, Ku Cheng-lun 谷正倫 , came personally to the station to greet him. He showed him a telegram from Chiang Kai-shek which said that Ch'en should be given every comfort and every encouragement to repent and join the Kuomintang, because of his brilliant history during the Northern Expedition. If he would swear allegiance now, Chiang promised him a good future.

Back in the early twenties, when Ch'en was a Whampoa cadet and took part in the engagement against Ch'en Chiung-ming, he was close to Chiang. During the battle one Kuomintang division was routed by Ch'en Chiung-ming's forces and fled in panic, past Ch'en Keng and Chiang Kai-shek, on the road. Chiang sent Ch'en Keng to the front to order the division commander to shoot anyone who retreated. Ch'en did so, and the division attempted to counter-attack, but it was again defeated. Chiang then told Ch'en Keng himself to take command and regroup the troops, and personally to shoot anyone who ran away. He did that and he shot several soldiers, but the mass retreat was overwhelming, so that even officers turned and fled, leaving Ch'en and Chiang almost alone on the field.

At that time Chiang had just been freshly hailed in the city of Huichou as "commander-in-chief." Now he felt disgraced. He cried out, "I must die here! I have no face left to return to the people of Tung-kiang!"* Ch'en said to him, "Since you are the commander-in-chief, your death now could affect the whole revolution. This is after all but one division, and not a Whampoa-led division. Come back, we shall have another fight." The enemy was approaching, and only 500 meters separated them. Chiang would not move. Ch'en therefore picked him up and bodily carried

---

*East of the River; Canton.

him as far as the river, where they got aboard a boat and reached safety. After that Chiang treated Ch'en very warmly for a time, showered him with presents and gave him free access to his room.

One day when he was in Chiang's room he found on his desk a list of Whampoa cadets and leaders of the revolution. Beside the name of each Communist was a red circle. By his own name was a note: "This man is a Communist; not to be entrusted with field command." At this time he began to suspect Chiang's intentions. He had already been commissioned a brigadier general, with a field regiment, but now his orders were changed. He was to remain at Whampoa as an instructor. In August 1926 the party finally sent him to Russia, where he studied until December. He returned to China in time to rejoin T'ang Sheng-chih's forces in the Northern Expedition.

Ch'en was now brought before a hearing at Nanking. He was ordered to confess, admit his past mistakes, and give the details of communist work inside the Kuomintang and the army. "Traitor" Ku Shun-chang came in, to state that when he was first arrested he was more courageous and more obstinate than Ch'en, but after thinking it over had decided that he was really being foolish. He did not believe communism was possible in China. Chiang Kai-shek was right. Ku showed him many confessions that had been made by other former Communists. Ch'en swept them all from the table and dismissed Ku with the word "traitor."

4. "Temptations Resisted"

Next day a number of Whampoa graduates, his former classmates and students, came to see him. They wore gold-braided uniforms, displaying their high rank; their boots were shining. Chiang Kai-shek, they told him, would never kill a Whampoa cadet. He would welcome Ch'en back. They asked him how he liked the poor life in the Red Army and he spoke enthusiastically of their many victories--how easily they defeated Chiang's forces, and how he himself had recently captured General Yu Wei-chun, a former Red officer who had sold out to Chiang and was given a command in Honan. They grew annoyed as he told them these stories of Red glory, and they said,

"You dare to spread propaganda even here?" They had asked him the questions, he said; he was merely answering them truthfully. They left angrily.

A few days later Ch'en and the girl comrade and some others were moved to a better room and given fresh clothes. They did not know why, until Mme Sun Yat-sen came to see them, with Yang Ch'üan* 楊銓 , a Chinese woman comrade, and a foreign woman. Ch'en told them that they had been given special treatment to prepare for the visit, however. The warden was angry and after they left Ch'en was put in a dirty uncomfortable cell. It was at first completely dark. Then a light was turned on and he saw human bones, knives and guns on the wall. A man was pointing a gun at him. He repeated, "Confess! confess!"

Ch'en was then taken out, and his head was shaved.

Removed from the Nanking jail by gendarmes, Ch'en was next put on a boat which took him upriver. Soon he arrived at Nanchang, then the Generalissimo's headquarters. Here he was kept at the Ta-lu-shih, a hotel "occupied mainly by Chiang Kai-shek's spies." Chiang's secretary, Teng Wen-yi 登阝文 儀 , a former Red and a returned student from Moscow, came to talk with Ch'en. He repeated much the same thing Ku had said. The revolution was a failure; China needed unity and strong leadership; democracy was not practical here. He told Ch'en of "Hsien-sheng's" ("Mr.'s," i.e. Chiang's) reforms. For example, General Ho Cheng-sheng had been punished because he went to a prostitute; several magistrates had been shot for corruption; many new highways and railways were being built. Ch'en replied that the only roads and railways Chiang was building were to fight the Reds, not to help the people. Teng insisted that Chiang was really anti-Japanese and was preparing to fight in 1936. He said China was uniting under Whampoa leadership. The Paoting militarists had ruled China for more than thirty years, with only two or three thousand graduates; Whampoa's 10,000 graduates could rule China for eighty years. All, Kuomintang and Reds alike, had only to unite under Chiang, as sole leader. Chiang's ambition was to win back all the Whampoa cadets, away from the Reds; even if it was necessary, he would not kill them.

To all that persuasion Ch'en remained indifferent. When Teng left he told him Chiang would see him the next day. That evening Teng came and

---

*Then secretary of the Academia Sinica; he was soon afterward assassinated.

took him out to a Cantonese restaurant for a big meal. Ch'en had had a
bath but had refused to change clothes or be shaved. In the morning Teng
came over and brought him a copy of an order just issued by Chiang. It
called for the presentation of $50,000 to the family of Kuo Pen-sheng, a
Whampoa graduate and a former Red, who had turned coat and joined the
Generalissimo. He had just been killed by the Reds (during the Fourth
Extermination Campaign). Ch'en merely expressed his disgust with Kuo.
Teng still asked Ch'en to sign a manifesto saying that he had repented and
changed his mind. He would then be given command of any division in Chiang's
army that he preferred. If not, he could be chief of staff of the armies
then surrounding the Honan-Hupeh-Anhui (E-yü-wan) soviet districts. Some ten
divisions commanded by Wang Chun were there. Ch'en declined these offers.

5. Conversation Piece

That afternoon he was taken to see Chiang. Teng brought him a silk
gown, a hat and some shoes, and he wanted to have him shaved. He said it
wasn't polite of him to see "Hsien-sheng" in that condition. Ch'en replied
that it wasn't an interview that he had sought. Teng gave up and took him
just as he was. At headquarters Ch'en waited downstairs in a big room filled
with bodyguards. Finally he heard some leather shoes creaking on the stairs;
he looked up and saw Chiang. Ch'en covered his face with a paper and pre-
tended to sleep. Chiang asked for Ch'en and the bodyguards produced him.

Chiang politely asked how he was, what kind of trip he had had, how
he liked it here, how he came to be here. Ch'en replied that he had been
arrested and brought here, by Chiang.

Chiang asked how he could speak that way. They were old comrades from
Whampoa days. All Whampoa men now must unite to save the country. The
president of Whampoa would not kill any Whampoa man. The hsiao-chang
would not kill him. He understood Ch'en had just come from E-yü-wan. How
were things going there?

Ch'en: "Ma-ma hu-hu (fairly well)."

Chiang: "In these years the deaths of peasants killed in fighting the
bandits exceed 300,000. China cannot afford this. All this is caused by the
Red bandits."

Ch'en: "The Communists are not responsible for these deaths. The Kuomintang began the counter-revolution which is responsible."

Chiang: "Shame! You ought to repent, you ought to repent! but still the president will not kill you."

Ten or more bodyguards heard all this, and Chiang was furious. Ch'en expected a kick at any moment. Just then someone called Chiang and he left the room saying, "Teng will represent me in all future talks with you."

Teng conducted Ch'en back to the hotel and asked him what he intended to do.

Teng: "If Chiang releases you, will you return to the Red Army and tell other Whampoa students that Chiang would not kill them if they come back to him?"

Ch'en replied that he would not join the Kuomintang and he would never repudiate Marxism. Teng said he would return to Nanking and let him think it over. That was the last time Ch'en saw Teng.

6. Escape or -- ?

Back in Nanking, Ch'en was put in a tiny cell, where he was badly treated for a month. Then a "fascist officer" came to talk to him. He asked what conclusion Ch'en had reached, but Ch'en had not changed his mind. A week later he was shifted to a hotel and kept under surveillance. By now he had cut off his beard and was cleaned up.

> Here Ch'en's account became rather ambiguous. It seemed likely that he was permitted to escape for the reason Teng mentions above, but Ch'en evidently considered that the escape was genuine.

In the hotel room a comrade (evidently someone in the gendarmerie, who revealed himself as a secret Communist) appeared and said that since they intended to keep Ch'en in the hotel, now he could try to escape. That night two Communist party members helped him sneak out of the hotel. They led him to the house of a gendarme who was secretly a Communist. This gendarme then accompanied him to Shanghai and put him back in touch with the party, whose apparatus then took charge and smuggled him into Kiangsi.

On Ch'en's arrival at Juichin he became president of the Red Academy, a post which he held for about a year, or until the great retreat or Long March.

At the Chin Sha Chiang (River), during the Long March, Ch'en Keng and his cadets held an important bridge for five days, until the main forces of the Red Army arrived and drove off attacking White troops. This opened up the way to the Northwest. Throughout the March Ch'en led the cadets of the Red Academy, some of whom resumed their studies on their arrival in Shensi. Ch'en himself assumed command of the First Division when Lin Piao took over the academy.

Ch'en had a shy, boyish manner, red cheeks and a ready smile; he was good-looking by Western standards. He had large eyes and an un-Chinese, upturned nose.

This story may be of interest mainly because it is the only case known, to me at least, in any such detail which shows that by 1933-34 Chiang himself was using the tactics of kindly treatment and persuasion in an effort to win over Red officers--particularly Whampoa cadets. From this time on, if not earlier, he also sent messages to people like Chou En-lai, Yeh Chien-ying, and P'eng Teh-huai, offering them honors and rewards for abandoning the Communist cause. If he permitted Ch'en to return to Kiangsi to demonstrate his magnanimity--pour encourager les autres--the strategem was not very successful. As far as I know he never won over any important Red generals (with the exception of Kung Ho-ch'ung, captured in Szechwan and shot in 1955) during that period.

XIV. RED ARMY LOSSES ON THE LONG MARCH

The following is based on a conversation with Chou En-lai at Pao-an; diary record dated September 26, 1936.

Chou says that the greater part of the Red Army losses took place in Szechwan, Kweichow and Sikang. Losses due to actual fighting with the Kuomintang forces were less than those from fatigue, sickness, starvation and attacks from tribesmen.

About 90,000 armed men left Kiangsi with the main forces. Of these 45,000 had been "lost" by the time the Red Army crossed the Chin-sha River into Szechwan. Meanwhile Hsü Hsiang-ch'ien left the E-yü-wan area in 1934, with between 50,000 and 60,000 troops. When he had been in Szechwan six months he increased his forces to more than 100,000. Late in 1935 Ho Lung left Hunan with about 40,000 troops. He reached Sikang with not more than 20,000, more likely 15,000.

On the arrival of the three armies in Szechwan, therefore, the figures were roughly as follows:

	Left base with:	Reached Szechwan with:	Losses
Chu Teh - Mao - Chou	90,000	45,000	45,000
Hsu Hsiang-ch'ien - Chang	50,000	100,000 (+50,000)	none
Ho Lung - Hsiao K'e	40,000	15,000	25,000

A total of 160,000 men, of whom more than half were under Hsü Hsiang-ch'ien and Chang Kuo-t'ao, while the Kiangsi-Hunan forces had lost 70,000 men en route.

In 1935 the First Army Corps left Szechwan and arrived in Shen-pei with about 7,000 men. There it joined Liu Chih-tan's force of about 10,000. Hsü Hai-tung also came up from Honan in 1935 with 3,000 troops left out of a starting force of 8,000. New enlistments in Shen-pei, Shansi, Kansu and Linghsia resulted in approximately the following:

First Army Corps (arrived from Szechwan with):	7,000
Shen-pei troops under Liu Chih-tan (later used as replacements):	10,000
Hsü Hai-tung forces from E-yü-wan:	3,000
Shansi enlistments on 1935 expedition:	8,000
New enlistments in Shen-pei, and deserters from Manchurian and Mohammedan Armies:	7,000
Approximate strength of regular forces in Northwest now:	35,000
Partisans and Red Guards in all Shen-Kan-Ning:	30,000 (estimate)

Chou En-lai estimates the present strength of the Second Front and Fourth Front Armies now en route to north Kansu, all the survivors from the winter in Sikang, as between 40,000 and 50,000.* What, then, has happened to the rest of the troops? These figures seem to tell a fascinating story with the details as yet to be filled in:

		Left base with	1935	Reached Northwest in 1936 with	Unaccounted for
1.	Hsü Hsiang-ch'ien and Chang Kuo-t'ao	50,000	100,000		
2.	Chu Teh	90,000	45,000		
3.	Ho Lung	40,000	15,000	50,000	

    *Today their combined forces arriving in the Northwest were at most 50,000, according to Chou. If the peak strength of each command is combined we get a figure of 230,000 men. Subtracting from that the 7,000 men who reached Shensi with Mao - P'eng leaves a total of 223,000, and 173,000

		Left base with	1935	Reached Northwest in 1936 with	Unaccounted for
4.	Mao Tse-tung and P'eng	? ?	First Army Corps 1935	7,000	? ?
5.	Hsü Hai-tung	8,000		3,000	5,000

Forces added in Northwest:

	Left base with	1935	Reached Northwest in 1936 with	Unaccounted for
Shen-pei troops under Liu Chih-tan	10,000		60,000	178,000
New enlistments in Shansi	8,000			
Enlistments in Shen-pei and Kansu-Ninghsia		7,000		
		25,000		

This table suggests a total combined loss in all Red Armies over a little less than two years of about 180,000 men. Some of the diminution is accounted for by the fact that the Red Army is always made up of a certain percentage of forces who are expected to remain behind to lead partisan detachments. Chou suggested that about 40,000 men might have been left behind for this purpose along the whole route of the March from Kiangsi and north of the river, too, which would still leave 140,000 "lost."

The above figures would give the Red Army regulars a total strength of about 90,000 when the three front armies are combined. In addition, local troops and partisans, with very few arms, perhaps number as many as 35,000.

From my own observation and investigation of claims and counter-claims concerning different units I have seen in action, I would guess that the

Red Army commanders, like most Chinese commanders, overstate their numbers. They may not do so for the same reasons. For example, in most warlord armies officers are paid for so many "names," and this leads to "padding." In the Red Army officers receive the same pay as men, which is negligible, and there is no such thing as corruption or misappropriation of rank-and-file pay for personal enrichment. But exaggeration there is, for the purpose of misleading the enemy.

My guess would be that the present Red strength may not exceed 30,000 to 50,000 regulars, with no more than 30,000 rifles.

XV. THE FORMOSAN

Ts'ai Ch'ien 蔡乾 was born in 1908 in Changhua near Taichung, Taiwan (Formosa). His father was an accountant in a rice shop and a descendant of the three hundred Fukienese families who went to Taiwan with Koxinga, who led a rebellion there against the Manchus.

At the age of six Ts'ai Ch'ien entered primary school, studied Japanese, and graduated after eight years. He taught at the same school, in Changhua, for one year. In 1924 he came to Shanghai, financed partly by his father and partly by the Chinese Cultural Association of Taiwan. He attended Shanghai University, where Yü Yu-jen was president, in 1924-25.

In Shanghai Ts'ai studied sociology and learned something about Marxism. In December 1926 he returned to do propaganda work for the Chinese revolution in Taiwan, where he helped organize a left wing in the Cultural Association. In Shanghai he had already joined the Socialist Youth organization. Now the Cultural Association adopted a radical program. The Japanese learned of it and arrested ten of its leaders, all returned students from China, and twenty other youths. They were accused of being Communists.

Ts'ai Ch'ien himself was arrested in Taihoku in January 1927 and taken to prison. He was charged with communism, on the basis of radical literature found in his baggage, and was sentenced to a year in jail. In November he was paroled. He had been allowed a cell to himself and had not been badly treated in jail. The Cultural Association was allowed to send him food. Following his release Ts'ai worked on the Ta Tsun Shih Pao as a reporter.

In April 1928 a Communist party of Taiwan was organized by Japanese and Taiwanese students, in Shanghai. Ts'ai helped to set up cells in Taiwan. In Taihoku the Japanese police discovered their organization and arrested their leaders. In November 1928 Ts'ai left Taiwan for Amoy, where he worked in the Amoy branch of the Taiwan party. In February of that year he went to Changchou, Fukien, and became a teacher in the Shih-Ma Middle School. Three years later he secretly entered the soviet districts and helped the Reds prepare their attack on Changchou, which they occupied briefly. In May 1932 Ts'ai reached Juichin and joined the faculty of the Lenin Academy, where he taught sociology, land problems, etc. He then took over the work of the Anti-Imperialist League, being in charge of liaison with colonial peoples.

During the Long March Ts'ai served in the political department of the First Army Corps as a commissar. In Shensi he returned to his work as chairman of the Anti-Imperialist League--now re-named the Anti-Japanese League. In April he also became minister of the interior in the Northwest Soviet government.

Ts'ai's wife, a Formosan, was left behind in Kiangsi; he presumes she found her way to safety in Fukien.

Ts'ai Ch'ien reads and speaks Japanese as fluently as Chinese.

If he is still alive, Ts'ai may now be very prominent in, if not actually the head of , underground communist work in Formosa.

XVI. GENERAL P'ENG TEH-HUAI 彭德懷

ON CHINA AND THE WORLD SITUATION

I had four long interviews with General P'eng which covered his personal history, the history of his army from the time he joined the Reds, the strategy and tactics of partisan-guerrilla warfare, and the current politico-military situation. The first three subjects were pretty thoroughly reported in Red Star Over China, but the comments below were not used because of space limitations and because other more important and dramatic events had superseded them in value. Now they may be of some interest historically, as a reflection of the thinking of the high command of the Red Army and the party at this critical time of a transition in Communist policy. Remarks which seem to me redundant or purely hortatory or in the nature of a harangue have been omitted in this instance, as the full text is very long.

The following are extracts from an interview at Yu Wang Pao, Ninghsia province, on August 16, 1936.

"The political situation in China is one link in the whole world chain. The Chinese revolution has reached a new stage, with new characteristics. First, it is no longer isolated, because the conflict throughout the world between capitalist and socialist society is (everywhere) becoming more acute. At the same time, the conflict within the capitalist structure is also sharpening. The golden age of capitalism has already passed. America is a good example. In the capitalist countries the class struggle has intensified. In France, Germany, Spain and other European countries this struggle is conducted on a wide front. Capitalism in those countries has nearly exhausted its possibilities.

"Second, in colonial and semi-colonial countries the resistance and struggle against imperialist exploitation is increasing. In Abyssinia, India, China, Korea, Egypt and Palestine the struggle is reaching new depths and intensity.

"Third, the rivalry for colonies among the imperialist countries is increasing. Italy's annexation of Abyssinia has aroused the resentment of other imperialists. In Manchuria and China, Japanese imperialism conflicts deeply with the interests of British and American imperialism. This rivalry and jealousy among the imperialists weakens the whole system throughout the world.

"At present China is gradually losing its independence and becoming colonized. During this time the ruling class is being divided. Even among Chiang Kai-shek's clique there are splits, feuds, factions, cliques; every militarist has his own background. The officials of the Nanking government dislike their position and feel that there is no future for them. This is the beginning of the collapse of the whole ruling class. All the officials of the Kuomintang and in the pay of Chiang Kai-shek are in conflict, and the division among them indicates a greater and deeper decay of the ruling class. It becomes apparent that they are themselves dissatisfied with their own rule.

"Another fact which established the non-isolation of the Chinese revolution is the Soviet Union. The liquidation of classes has been completed, and economic crisis, bankruptcy, and social maladjustments have ended. The minorities in the Soviet Union have won genuine independence and emancipation. The proletariat of the world has been taught by this that the Soviet Union can be their model and that they must carry on their own struggle following that model. Only in this way can they win freedom and assure peace. Especially in China the example of the Soviet Union has had a tremendously stimulating effect. Because of the contrast between Soviet policies and those of the imperialists, the Chinese people realize that the Soviet Union is the only country opposed to exploitation and determined to protect the interests of the weak and small countries and of minorities. [P'eng had not been to the U.S.S.R.]

"The Outer Mongolian-Soviet pact (non-aggression) had a very stimulating effect, showing the masses that the Soviet Union is the genuine friend of minorities of China. Chiang Kai-shek and the traitors made a protest over this pact. In reply, the Soviet Union frankly pointed out the failure of the Kuomintang to offer any resistance in Manchuria, in North China, and against Japanese smuggling, declaring that the Soviet Union had no ambitions to annex Outer Mongolia, and that it clearly recognized it as part of China. The Chinese masses thus more clearly understood the real role of Chiang and the Kuomintang, and at the same time their understanding of Soviet policies increased and their feeling of friendship deepened.*

---

*I presume these comments on Outer Mongolia were in answer to questions I raised, but I now have no record of the latter.

"Since the failure of the Great Revolution ten years have passed. What has Chiang Kai-shek accomplished for the people, the masses, and the capitalists? To the people Chiang has brought heavy taxes and a slave future. To the capitalists the Kuomintang and Chiang's rule have brought crisis and bankruptcy. To the peasantry Chiang has brought ruination of the agrarian economy . . . . During the Long March we passed Kwangsi, Kweichow, Yunnan, Szechwan and other provinces and witnessed at first hand the living conditions of the peasantry. In winter, when the snow was still heavy, people had no clothes to wear. Women who had already passed twenty still had no trousers to put on. Peasants could not manage to get even one meal a day. These conditions prevailed in all provinces we passed, so that the majority of peasants were driven down the road of death. 'There is no way to heaven, no door to hell.' This is the 'construction' program of the Kuomintang, this the 'virtue' of the Kuomintang . . .

"Chiang Kai-shek and the traitors defame the Chinese people, saying that they are mostly illiterate, but up to the present the traitors who sell out the nation are mostly educated and returned students from Japan. Chiang is a returned student from Japan; so is Yin Ju-keng 殷汝耕 (puppet in East Hopei) . . . . But the Chinese masses know that if we don't resist when imperialists invade China there is no method that can make construction possible, raise the cultural level of the people, enrich peasant economy, etc. If China wants to accomplish these tasks, the only way is to organize a National Defense Government, as the Chinese Communist Party has advocated. This expressed the demand of the majority of the Chinese people, namely: the United Front against Japanese imperialism. Even Chiang's own generals have expressed their ideas about that. In 1932, when General Ch'en Ch'eng was surrounding Kiangsi while the Japanese were occupying Manchuria, he said, 'The Chinese enemy is not the Red Army, but the Japanese. We must unite with them to fight Japan.' Many other generals made the same demand. Chiang's reply was, 'If anyone wants to make war with Japan and cease war on the Red Army, the answer is death to him!'

"So General Hu Tsung-nan expressed his view about continued war against the Reds very sadly. 'To fight the Reds,' he said, 'is a life sentence.' Others said, 'To oppose the Reds is to clear a road for the Japanese' . . . .

When the Nineteenth Route Army fought the Shanghai war Chiang sent his own troops to disarm them . . . . When the Nineteenth Route Army established the People's Government in Fukien, Chiang sent more than ten divisions to destroy it. More recently, when Kwantung and Kwangsi called upon the nation to resist Japan, Chiang divided them—by money, bribes, etc. The Chinese Red Army since the September 18th Incident has declared to the whole country that it is willing to cooperate with any armed forces to resist Japan . . . . When the Red Army crossed the Yellow River, declaring that it would enter Hopei to fight Japan, Chiang Kai-shek promptly sent his troops to construct fortifications and to force other troops to attack the Red Army base in Shensi . . . .

"After our retreat (from Shansi, in May 1936) we proposed to Nanking to cease war for one month. At the same time delegates were sent, advocating the alliance of all forces for war against Japan. No reply was received and our delegates were arrested in Shansi. The delegate to Nanking has not been heard of since. Chiang gave his reply by continued attack; several divisions belonging to T'ang En-po 湯恩伯 entered Shensi to fight us. Chiang's deceit ought to be fully realized under these circumstances. Formerly Chiang said that the Kuomintang was really anti-Japanese but could not resist because of the Reds in their rear. To say now that the Reds are destroying Chiang's rear is ridiculous, for they have no contact. On the contrary, it was Kuomintang troops that blocked the Reds from fighting Japan. While the Red Army was moving north to fight Japan, Chiang was withdrawing from North China and possible contact with Japanese troops . . . ."

Edgar Snow: "Do you think it is impossible, then, that the Nanking government under Chiang Kai-shek will in the future resist Japan?"

P'eng Teh-huai: "We really hope that Nanking will cooperate with us, but we fear that this cannot be realized . . . Nanking has accepted the Three Principles of Hirota [Japanese foreign minister] and two of these principles make resistance out of the question. First, all anti-Japanese activity must be suppressed; second, Japanese imperialism and the Nanking government must form a united front against communism. Under continued pressure, however, the danger of enslavement by Japan may bring about a division at Nanking and swing one part of the Kuomintang on the side of the (national) anti-Japanese front."

Q. "Now that the Fourth Army under Chu Teh has reached Kansu, what is the probable effect on the Northwest military and political situation?"

A. "Chiang must obey the Hirota Principles; therefore he must oppose the Red concentration. In this he will fail. The possibilities (as a result of the unification of Red forces) are bright because (1) nine years of struggle have given the Red Army experience and fighting ability surpassing all other forces in China; (2) our political mission now is to resist Japan, and this mission raises still higher the determination of our Red fighters to destroy Chiang's opposition; (3) Red slogans and policies are clear, and appeal to the majority of the White troops; (4) we have crossed the most difficult passes and rivers of China and have already reached a richer district, easier to maneuver in. The greatest difficulties are now behind us . . . ."

P'eng then pointed out favorable factors in the Northwest, and the various stages of discontent among the different armies and populations there.

Q. "If a united front is achieved here between the Red Army, the Manchurian armies, the Mohammedans, and Sung Che-yüan's 宋哲元 troops, is it possible and advisable to begin resistance to Japan at once, or must a united front be achieved throughout the whole country first?"

A. "It is quite possible to form a united front not only with the troops you mention but also with certain military leaders and the mass of the soldiers in Shansi . . . . As Japanese imperialism will use its own forces to attack the united front in the Northwest, it is quite clear that resistance is the only possible policy. In practice it is probably impossible to achieve a national united front before resistance begins. The Red Army is the vanguard . . . ."

P'eng next answered questions on China's preparedness, the strategy and tactics of a war with Japan, prospects of outside help, etc.

XVII. WITH THE RED ARMY
Fragments from a Travel Diary

<u>August 5, 1936.</u> <u>Somewhere in Kansu.</u>

Two days of marching over narrow trails through an endless dry river bed. The country is arid, broken up, the hills thinly grassed, and there are few trees. Shallow, clay-covered ravines occasionally have a little brackish water in them, not fit to drink. There are few habitations of any kind; we have not passed a village since we left Wu-chi Chen. On the sides of the hills, near cultivated patches here and there, are <u>yao-fang</u>, or man-made caves. Occasionally there is a mud-walled house with its roof made of roughhewn willow trees or alders. These are the houses of landlords who have fled. There are no articles from the outside world for sale here; no books, pictures, glass, tin--or metals of any kind except the iron in ploughs or a few primitive tools.

Here on the Shensi-Kansu border people live in loess hills just as their ancestors must have lived 5,000 years ago. Men wear their hair long and braided, and all the women have bound feet. They rarely bathe. It is said that a Shensi native is clean twice in his life: on his wedding day when he takes a bath; and on his burial day, when he is given one. They speak a strange dialect scarcely intelligible to the "foreign invaders" (the Reds). In their caves they keep their mules, horses, goats, sheep, pigs and chickens, and they sleep in the midst of them. On the Kansu border sheep are fairly plentiful: a chicken costs twenty cents,* a sheep three dollars and a pig (theoretically) a dollar. It is fairly easy to buy a sheep, but the natives hide their pigs and chickens, and bring them out only if you have something to barter. They use paper money to buy salt, cloth and opium, but otherwise it has little value for them. The nearest cooperative is several hundred <u>li</u> distant.

<u>August 26, 1936.</u> <u>Yu-wang-hsien, Kansu.</u>

I left Yu-wang-pao at 7:30 after breakfasting with P'eng Teh-huai, Li Fu-ch'ün 李富春 and others. The First Division had given me a black pony captured from Ma Hung-pin 馬鴻賓 , and I rode this fine beast across

---

*Chinese national currency--then about U.S. $0.06.

a plain as level as a table. There were miles of grassland here, much of it former farmland now gone back to pasture after the Mohammedan rebellion and the droughts and famines of the past two decades. We passed a small herd of gazelles moving with incredible grace and speed. What population remains today is almost entirely Mohammedan. The architecture of the scattered villages has a Moorish flavor--the roofs, the wide gates, and the wide court-yards swept immaculately clean--in contrast to the slovenliness of Shensi.

Here in Yu-wang-hsien the Fifteenth Army Corps under Hsü Hai-tung makes its bivouac. Hsü had sent a platoon of his men, mounted on little Mongolian ponies, to meet us--Wang Ju-mei,* Ma Hai-teh, Fu Chin-kuei and myself. We covered the seventy li quickly, running our horses about half the way. Toward noon Wang's cinchstrap slipped, his horse bolted straight for the walled town and did not stop till he reached it. Wang somehow hung on to the bitter end--a true hero, for it was almost his first ride.

A welcoming committee stood outside the gates between banners which said: "Welcome to the American international journalist to investigate the soviet districts." Bugles played as we entered the massive walls dotted with townspeople come to witness the arrival of the foreign devils. A well-built Mohammedan temple stood just outside the south gate; beyond the north gate was another. Between these gates stretched a street of shops ending in two pretty towers, one of which housed a theater.

Inside the city the troops of the Seventy-third, Seventy-fifth and Seventy-eighth Divisions were lined up by companies, each coming to attention and singing their songs or shouting slogans as we rode past. Battalion and regimental flags unfurled, more bugles blew, orderlies dashed ahead of us. At the south end of town we were met by General Hsü Hai-tung and his staff, lined up before a three-stored tower, where quarters were provided for us. Below was a bomb-proof shelter.

Under the topmost tower Hsü improvised an apartment of two rooms, furnished with beds made of wooden doors. The place was spotlessly clean. On a table were some apples, sugar--and coffee! From the balcony you could see every corner of the city, and beyond it as far as the walls of Weichow,

---

*Wang Ju-mei, a Yenching graduate, came to the Northwest after I arrived there. He is called Huang Hua today and is an official in the foreign office under Chou En-lai.

forty <u>li</u> away. In this clear air nothing broke the view for miles, and
through Hsü's glasses I could easily make out Ma Hung-k'uei's (White) soldiers
on the walls of Weichow. In another direction, to the northwest, some twenty-
five <u>li</u> away, you could see the Communists' utmost <u>pao-lei</u>, or pillbox.

August 27. Yu-wang-hsien.

I talked all morning with Hsü Hai-tung and then all afternoon till
five and after, while he unfolded the amazing story of the Fourth Red Army
in the Hupeh-Honan-Anhui district—the E-yü-wan republic. Hsü, a battered
veteran who has been wounded eight times, bounces with as much unspent energy
as the phenomenal P'eng Teh-huai. Both men are obviously superglandular.
About Hsü there is something appealingly naive, impulsive and at the same
time shy. He blushes easily. He has two front teeth missing as a result of
a fall from a horse, and when he smiles, which is often, the gap seems to
emphasize the mixture of childlike sincerity and modesty and bashfulness.
His figure is slight, wiry and tough; he is proud of his strength and marks-
manship, which he likes to demonstrate. He eats little and is hardly aware
of what he eats. He rises every day at 4:00. His energy and attention to
detail are reflected in the (good physical) condition of his army and its
neatness and discipline.

The Red Army I am seeing here does not behave much like the conven-
tional idea of a revolutionary army. The long history of struggle has made
orderly, disciplined veterans even of the teenaged officers.

August 30. Yu-wang-hsien.

The Fifteenth Army Corps began moving westward today. Bugles sounded
very early this morning and kept blowing steadily until we left. By that
time the main forces were already on the road. Hsü, Cheng, Wang and other
members of the staff stayed with us and we all left the city together. How
smoothly, how simply, these thousands of men moved out of the city—an
excellent example of the efficiency of Red organization. Yesterday afternoon
I visited the different regimental headquarters of this command and saw that
most of the troops were still settled down as if for a long stay. By morning
everything—maps, books, tools, ammunition, food, weapons—was packed on the

backs of mules and men and already far ahead of us.

Hsü Hai-tung had spent the whole previous evening with us, as the army prepared to advance. You would not have thought that it was any more complicated to move 8,000 men out of the city than for an individual to take a walk. Yet their destination is 200 li to the west, and they expect resistance as they forge open a road to link the soviet bases here with the oncoming armies of Chu Teh, moving up from the south. Plans for the march were completed days ago, I was told; the Red Army knew exactly where it would encamp on each succeeding day. For the past four days peasants moving back and forth across no-man's land had been detained, in order to prevent news of the Reds' imminent departure from reaching the enemy. Now their advance was unexpected, and unopposed.

As we walked out across the grassy ocean of the plain this morning, tailing the rear guard, a long serpentine of men disappeared over the horizon. Suddenly a bugled signal was given. The whole army left the road and simply melted into the grasslands, dispersing under their grass-ringed hats for air-raid practice. It was perfect camouflage; from 100 yards away you could not tell men from the atolls of bunch grass. Even the pack animals were hidden by their blankets of woven grass.

August 31.

At a mud fort in the road, or the path that is called a road, we came to a fork, and Hsü went southward and I continued west. The old fort looked like one of those desert outposts where the French Foreign Legion is always shooting down the Arabs. Here I told Hsü and his staff goodbye. The staff went on, but to my surprise Hsü got off his horse and walked along hand in hand with me for a mile, talking about his army, its problems, the condition of the men, how to keep them fed and warmly clad in the coming winter. "Can't you give us some advice on how to improve?" he demanded. "We are only ignorant peasants; we know nothing of the outside world." He said he hoped more Americans would come to see the Red Army and work with it. He asked me to return; he repeatedly asked this. I was much moved by his obvious sincerity. He kept saying that he was "so honored" to have me come such a very great distance to see him and his men and hear their story to tell the world.

"We shall meet again!" he said, as at last he stopped and turned to go. "We shall certainly meet again!" Now to my surprise he took a black jade snuff bottle from his pocket and said, "Please take this as a souvenir from the Fifteenth Army and myself. My men want you to have it so that you will not forget us. It once belonged to a Mongolian prince and is famous among the peasants all over here. Take it and you will return home safely." With that he got on his horse, saluted and rode off.

After leaving Hsü I rode over to the First Army Corps headquarters, where I had dinner with P'eng Teh-huai.

September 1, 1936.

We left Yu-wang-pao this morning at six, after bugles had sounded since three. Yesterday afternoon I stood by the great stone gate of the city watching the First Army Corps depart for Hai-yuan, farther west. The long caravan of men and animals filed past, stretching out over four or five _li_. The arms were mostly first class in this, the pick of the Red Army. They included recent types of German and Czech rifles, British automatic rifles, machine guns, Mausers, and artillery batteries with shells tenderly carried in canvas bags. Smaller articles showed more improvisation: camp stoves, kettles, buckets, pots and pans all made of Standard Oil or other kinds of oil cans.

Next, the players and minstrels went by with their portable drops and props, sharing a mule or two between them, and singing. The gramophone they carried reminded me of one presented to us during our stay in Ho-lien-wan. It had two French records. One had the "Marseillaise" on one side and "Tipperary" on the other. The second record was a French comedy song, one of those laughing things. Though the Reds couldn't understand French they understood the spirit of this, and the laughter. The whole army could be sent into paroxyms by it. The "little devils" listened by the hour and mimicked it and cried their eyes out laughing. They never could figure, however, where the man in the box was hiding.

P'eng made all preparations to leave in an hour. By five o'clock the headquarters guard, about five hundred men, including cavalry, was ready and waiting below. P'eng packed his few shirts and pants, some maps, a telephone and batteries, into two tin boxes. He was then ready for the road. We had breakfast together, ate several melons each, and then rode off across rounded mountains and uninhabited plateau, but even the herds of sheep and goats seen elsewhere were absent here.

One saw frequent packs of gazelles, beautiful in their wild swift flight, gallop like dust clouds across the landscape. At times they completely encircled us from a distance of a mile or more; then, having satisfied their curiosity, they vanished as quickly and mysteriously as they had gathered.

September 9. Cheng-chia-wu, Kansu.

Reached here early in the afternoon, a seventy-_li_ march. My pony is exhausted, having been on the road five days without a rest.

The way led through grassy meadows spotted with wild flowers, purple and pale green asters, some very large and beautiful thistles and a dark crimson flower splashed like blood on the green hills. Gazelles were still numerous and overhead the sky was full of eagles,* some with a wing span of five or six feet. There were many larks, red-winged blackbirds, magpies and thrushes; the meadows were shrill with their swarming thousands. Along the way I saw several herds of three or four hundred sheep. Now and then wild horses raced across the far horizon. Once, high in the air, two eagles fought over a piece of carrion of some kind, tearing at each other and with their big wings fanning furiously.

We came upon a small Mohammedan village tucked into a narrow valley, the only settlement of the kind seen all day, and there we had our lunch. Fu Chin-kuei** and I sat under a tree overlooking the broad plain and watched the gazelles gallop over distant ridges, hazy in the noon sun. As we sat there filled with the sense of beauty and space of the grasslands, and the wonder and variety of China, Fu began talking to me of his childhood and how he had joined the Red Army.

---

*Could they have been buzzards?
**Fu was more than a bodyguard, but not quite an official. He was a kind of _kuan-shih-ti_ or steward for me, a companion but not a servant, a manager but not an interpreter.

He came, Fu said, from a village in south Kiangsi "where rice was so plentiful even the poorest man ate it." You could buy several _tan_ for a dollar. Still, in his home they were desperately poor and always in debt: even rice as a steady diet can become tiresome; where we were now that might not seem possible. Fu heard of a place called Ching-an, in central Kiangsi, and only two days from his village by a steam launch which traveled the nearby river. He often went to the wharf and asked the boatman about Ching-an. There was a thing called "electricity." For five _tiao_ of cash he could get to Ching-an and see that thing for himself.

Fu gradually amassed five _tiao_ and took the boat to Ching-an, and it was indeed an interesting place. He got a job in a weaving mill and made more money than he had ever seen. True, he had to spend it all because food and lodging were so expensive; but he had enough for an occasional night at the hot bath house, he saw the electric lights, he became a worker, and he even learned a few characters. When the revolution came he was popular among the younger workers and the Communist Youth organization approached him and taught him Marxism. He then organized a Communist Youth branch among the workers. They understood that the revolution was against landlords and the rich and that was enough for them. Fu became known as a youth leader.

After the counter-revolution scores of young people were arrested in Ching-an. Many were killed. Fu was put in jail, but over 500 workers from the mill signed a petition asking for his life, begging that he be released, and swearing that he was not a Communist. This was published in a local paper and he was eventually freed. Fu went back to work at the mill and did secret party work. When the Red Army captured Ching-an, in 1930, Fu was one of 6,000 workers who joined it. For a month the factories were under Communist control. Wages were quadrupled, every worker was given a bonus (Fu himself got thirty dollars), and for days the Red Army gave them feasts of pork, mutton and beef seized from the landlords. There were plays every night, and singing till everyone was hoarse. It was a "wonderful experience." But not so wonderful for the landlords. Several hundred were captured by the Reds and taken to the hsien city.

Now, according to Fu, the landlords, together with many captured White officers, were invited to a feast. They were given quantities of wine, in the traditional preparation for execution. Fu remembers that eighty or ninety dollars worth of <u>kaoliang</u> wine was consumed that night. Then they were all killed.

This was in 1930, said Fu, when the Red Army was still "dominated by the Li Li-san line." The "Trotskyists" urged a "ruthless war on the landlords and capitalists, a terror." Shortly afterward Li Li-san was deposed and the party line changed to its "present moderation." The bitterness of the White terror during the counter-revolution was fresh in the Communists' thought and they were in no mood for softness toward usurers and landlord allies of Chiang, said Fu. He (Fu) joined the Red Army at that time and has been with it ever since.

Fu has the polish and aplomb of a college graduate, though he is entirely self-taught and educated by the Red Army. He is naturally intelligent, capable and shrewd; he has patience, is very observant, and courageous. One would hardly believe he was a totally illiterate peasant a few years ago.

September 16. <u>Hung-teh-ch'eng.</u>

. . . . In general one does not get the impression here of a people at war (except at the very front) with an army in movement.

There is no violence practiced upon the peasantry; at any rate, I have not seen it. I have not seen even a fist fight between soldier and civilian, or between civilians or between soldiers. I have seen no cases of attack on women, who move about, both old and young, in seeming freedom. I have seen comely young girls sit down beside bellows and pump the ancient instrument cheerfully for an hour or more to cook the soldiers' dinner, talking and joking with them meanwhile. During my stay here I have never seen a child struck nor an old man abused.

Near Ho-lien-wan I saw a family of landlords under arrest. They went part of the way along a mule road with us. There was the father, two sons and the mother. The latter was a stout woman of about forty-five. None of them was chained and the mother sat on a donkey on top of a pile of bedding and other belongings. She continually cursed the young soldiers who were guarding them; they laughed and joked back at her. The father, a poorly dressed man, walked along glumly and his two sons followed silently. The soldiers said, in answer to my question, that they were being taken to Ho-lien-wan for "investigation."

Besides these people, a Kuomintang tax collector (at Yu-wang-pao) and some "deserters" (half a dozen) digging ditches and latrines, I have seen only one other political prisoner in the soviet districts. One morning in Pao-an I passed several soldiers leading a young man wearing soiled cotton garments, with a look of despair on his peasant face. I learned that he was a "confessed spy," who had been a member of the district soviet revolutionary committee. He had been caught sending out reports to the Kuomintang (as I was told). Later on I saw him in the Pao-an jail, a stone cave in the hills.*

September 20. Wu-chi Chen.

Traveled ninety li today along a road which mostly followed a river bed and brought us here at dusk.

Just out of Tieh-ping Cheng, as we came upon the fields in the early dawn, a heavy white dew lay everywhere and a dense fog cloaked most of the valley. But slowly faint bars of sunshine broke through and struck the hillsides, turning the grass silver. The scrubby little trees sparkled like the jade trees Peking artisans make from glass and semi-precious stones.

At a turn in the road we came upon a large field of melons touched by this magic. They glistened like gems against the frosty earth. An old farmer, out early sampling them himself, offered me one and to my surprise it was more delicious than any melon I ever tasted. It was sweet, fresh and cold and the flesh was ruby against the white rind. We bought a dozen and ate them on the spot. Then, refreshed, we rode away happily "steeped," as it were, on the "foggy honey dew."

---

* I had intended to return and interview him, but left before I could get around to it.

XVIII. ON THE ROAD BACK

October 12, 1936.

I left Pao-an at about 9:00 A.M. bound for the highway to Sian. Everyone came out to say goodbye except Mao, who was still asleep. Lu Ting-yi walked me through the city gate and as far as the Red Academy. Down below, on the river's edge, Lin Piao and Lo Fu were lecturing to classes in the open air. They all stopped and rose and waved and shouted "Yi p'ing hao lu!" and "Shih Lo T'ung-chih, Wan Sui!" as I rode off. The "t'ung-chih" was just courtesy-talk, but a lump rose in my throat as I wondered how many of these youths would come out of there alive.

Ma Hung-k'uei, my horse, was lean with many days of travel and rationing on cornstalks and grass, but now he trotted briskly ahead of our small cavalcade all day. We followed the Pao-an River till sunset when we reached this halt at ____ Shan. But it isn't a mountain at all; we are in a farmhouse below a huge sandstone hill which towers 200 feet straight up from the stream. It looks like a giant beehive, with its hundreds of caves hollowed out from the stone, standing one on another above the single road which leads to the summit. An ancient temple crowns the hill; beside it is a house where the magistrate lived. These stone-cave settlements are numerous along the river, but this is the largest I have seen. The Red Army Academy was quartered in one.

Some of these yao-fang are surprisingly commodious and their inner walls are finely finished, their floors laid with brick or wood. With their heavy natural insulation they make warm homes in winter and cool ones in summer. They are impregnable forts against anything but a heavily-armed assault. They are deserted now, except for a few Red guards.

There is little to eat hereabouts, but our farmer-host was persuaded to sell us a chicken. With some pai-ts'ai and hsiao-mi rolls, which we had brought from Pao-an, it was a banquet, as we had had nothing to eat since morning. After dinner we sat on the peasant's k'ang and Fu Chin-kuei persuaded him to play his shansi, a long banjo-like instrument which resembles a samisen. (Perhaps the samisen was patterned after it.) Every Shensi household has a shansi, says Fu. A home-made shansi and a home-made rifle are the two necessities for setting up a household in Shensi.

The young peasant, our host, wore a turban of white towelling. He sat, very dignified, on his woolen rug made in Tingpien, his two bare feet tucked under him on the k'ang. His young wife sat beside him, also barefooted, nursing an infant at her full brown breast. Another brat crawled along papa's leg and pulled his big toes in wonder. His songs had a queer melancholy and seemed to come from far back in man's memory and fitted into this weird country quite exactly.

Peppers hung drying in the doorway; there were piles of pumpkins in a little storeroom beyond, and you could see bins of squash, turnips and hsiao-mi (millet). They were getting ready for the winter. Pigs, large and fat, ambled between the legs of the soldiers as they stood listening to the songs. Some of the Shenpei men joined in when they knew the words to his music.

October 13.

We are in a small village with a broken-down temple and many young and broken-footed women. In the house where we are quartered are four women-- three daughters-in-law and one despotic mother-in-law. It's quite evident the revolution has not freed the women from a "mother-in-law tyranny." The man of the house came round with his small son, who had a badly infected finger, and wanted help. There was nothing I could do except tell him to wash it and keep it clean. These people haven't any idea of a connection between dirt and disease.

We had a feast: fried cabbage, hashed brown potatoes (!) at my insistence, fried chicken, steamed bread and turnips. Everybody shouted "Hao! Hsiang!" It was really excellent fare.

"K'u?" asked a young soldier, jesting. "Pu k'u," said I. What, I asked him, was really "bitter"? Not to have bread and potatoes, but to feed only on hsiao-mi?

"No, that can't be reckoned bitter," he replied. "If there's no rice we eat bread, no bread we eat hsiao-mi, no hsiao-mi we eat corn, no corn we eat potatoes, no potatoes we eat cabbage, no cabbage we drink hot water, no hot water we drink cold water. But if there's no water at all? Shih-ti, that's bitter!"

There is a festive air around the village now in October, with the red and green peppers drying everywhere, and the green cabbage and golden pumpkins lying in the autumnal sun.

We are put up, wherever we stop, by the P'in-min-hui, the Poor People's League. There is at least one representative in every village.

October 14.

We stopped in a hut high up on a mountainside overlooking a green wooded valley, where I saw my first rice field since leaving Fushih. The owner of this tumble-down place is a Szechwanese who came here twenty years ago. He called his farm "twenty mou high" as it slanted down the hill and was precarious to cultivate. You had to be a pen-ti-jen (native), he explained, to get level land; as a foreigner he was strictly ruled out. Across the valley now was a farmer with one hundred mou of beautiful rice land, but he (our host) was just "poor Chang" of the P'in-min-hui. Nevertheless, "poor Chang" produced some eggs (everywhere very scarce) for us, several chickens, some potatoes and cabbage. Again we feasted, especially after Chang brought out some tou-tou yu-t'ang, an excellent bean-oil soup of his own concoction made of hsiao-mi, beans, bean oil and peppers. He proffered it to me modestly and beamed when I asked for more.

We (Fu Chin-kuei and our two soldiers) slept in a storage room hung with the farmer's scant winter provisions--garlic, beans, turnips, onions, cabbage, potatoes, a bit of rice and a smell of opium.

After dinner, when I was eating his bean soup, the farmer told me that three of his sons were soldiers: one was in the Red Army, Fifteenth Corps, cavalry regiment; a second was in the Red Guards; and the third was a ma-fu with a headquarters company. He had two younger sons. His one daughter squatted on the k'ang beside his wife and his sister.

October 15.

Today we did sixty li to a place called Fu-ts'un. The trip took us through wild country where all day we did not pass a house. Here the hills were interminable and thickly wooded and the brown rust of autumn lay everywhere around us. We saw many pheasant, a few deer and wild goats and wild pigs--and two tigers streaking from one thicket to another, far out of range.

We all fired at them and our shots fell short; we scolded ourselves for wasting ammunition, and laughed. The whole day was one of sheer beauty, an immense comfort to the eyes after months and months of barren hills and deserted valleys.

Yet even here were signs of desolation, and ruins from nameless centuries of the past. Fu-ts'un itself now held but a dozen families; all around lay the debris of a far larger settlement. First was the ruin of an old city wall, which certainly must have surrounded a considerable town; beyond, weed-grown streets and the rubble of countless houses littered what once may have been the suburb of a still larger place. We ourselves stayed in a cluster of half-house half-cave dwellings on the hill.

Here again our host was the local head of the P'in-min-hui. He was a bright young farmer who said that he had only two days before returned from Fu-hsiang, a village on the Sian highway toward which we are aiming. There he had been stopped by some of Yang Hu-ch'eng's soldiers and accused of being a "Red." His friends had warned him, however, and he had been ready for them with a good story. They had let him go. He reported that Yang's troops, some three or four regiments, held the road from Fu-hsiang to the outskirts of Sian. No one could travel without a pass, and a pass cost three or four dollars. If you didn't have it the soldiers would take what they pleased from you: money, clothes, food or anything you might have. Many peasants were being killed by Yang's men, as alleged Reds. Peasants now avoid the highway and travel at night by the small mountain roads.

October 16, 17, 18, 19. An-chia-pan.

Loafed here for four days and at least learned some new words. I have learned more Chinese on this trip, without anybody along who knows even a few words of English, than in two years of (desultory) study. I know everybody in the village by now.

My host here said he wanted my jacket (sheepskin lined) and I offered it to him, but he refused. I won't need it after I leave here, I told him; but he said he was joking. I discovered that he is a party member and has been a partisan leader in this district for five years. He really did have nothing--no possessions at all to show for all that fighting. He had his

young wife and a child with him. One day we sat on the k'ang and talked for
three hours. He told me that recently they went to the very edge of an en-
campment of White troops and sang songs to them, women and men together,
with one man playing a shansi. He sang several of the songs to me, full of
appeals and political and patriotic sentiments, asking the soldiers to come
over "to the people's side." Gradually, by twos and threes, the soldiers
began to drift over to them. Then they heard orders shouted to fire on them
in the darkness, but the soldiers fired in the air and no one was hurt.
These were Yang Hu-ch'eng's troops, but now they have been withdrawn and
been replaced by well-paid tough professional bandits of the Ke-lao-hui,
which has formed the backbone of Yang's ex-bandit army.

Here the peasants are amazed at the sight of a foreigner. The
word has traveled fast and people come from miles distant to have a look at
me. Many have invited me to visit their homes, to dine with them. Among
my visitors is a young girl of the partisans, armed and smiling, but just as
astonished at the sight as the others. I asked her if there were many landlords left hereabouts. She said pu-tuo (not many); they have fled. On the
other front they have all returned and some land has been given back to them,
in accordance with the new policy.

October 19, 1936. Tungpei Front.

I was escorted here this morning by twenty Red soldiers and found Pien
Chang-wu 邊彰武 waiting for me. Pien was the first Red officer I met
when I came into An-sai and now he was seeing me through to the "White"
world. He personally took me across no-man's-land and led me up to a few
Manchurian soldiers waiting on the plain. They were led by an immaculate
young officer wearing a gold sword and white gloves, and carrying a vacuum
flask. We exchanged greetings; I shook hands with Pien and he turned and
marched back across the plain.

The Tungpei officer and his squad led me to their regimental commander,
with whom I dined. The next morning General Ho Chu-kuo 何柱國 came to
call on me and we spoke for an hour or so before I left for Sian by truck.
Ho asked many questions about the Reds, their morale, equipment, policy and
the degree of their patriotism and determination to fight Japan. He seemed

pleased with what I told him. He expressed his impatience with the delay
in reaching an agreement to end the civil war.

That day I was put aboard a Tungpei army truck by the white-gloved
officer, who accompanied me right to the doors of the house, inside Sianfu,
where I was quartered at the orders of Chang Hsüeh-liang.

XIX. PRESIDENT ROOSEVELT ON CHINA

On February 24, 1942 I was in Washington trying to get a priority to fly by clipper ship to Africa as a war correspondent. While I sat in the office of Wayne Coy, a White House administrative assistant, word came to him that Mr. Roosevelt would like to see me. That afternoon I went to the Oval Room, where the President greeted me, saying that he knew me from Red Star Over China and my reports in the Saturday Evening Post. We spoke for nearly an hour, chiefly about the Far East. I called on him again when I was home on leave in 1944; the date was May 26. On my return to Russia I wrote to him several times, at his suggestion. During my next trip to Washington I visited him for the last time, on March 3, 1945, the day after he made his report to Congress on the Yalta Conference.

I kept fairly careful notes of those off-the-record talks, and later wrote them up in a personal paper which runs to more than 10,000 words. Most of this is of purely private interest today, but here and there a remark occurs which may be of some use to students of the period. The dialogue did not occur in the exact sequence presented here, of course; the extracts have been selected and condensed, with my own comment, to present as coherent an account as possible of rather desultory talk in which F.D.R. expressed himself on China in only a very limited way.

It was apparent to me that President Roosevelt was aware, even in 1942, that Chiang Kai-shek's regime lacked united and enthusiastic popular support. He genuinely desired that our aid might be useful in bringing about social, economic and political progress in China. For example, he asked me what we could do to help the people of China, as distinct from the government. On February 24, 1942 I spoke at considerable length about Chinese Industrial Cooperatives and the immediate and potential usefulness of this method of production to combat inflation, to help China attain self-sufficiency in consumer goods, and to establish some new economic basis for political democracy in the country.

Mr. Roosevelt was especially interested when I pointed out that "Indusco" was the only wartime organization (other than the Red Cross) able to operate in both Kuomintang and Communist-held areas. He seemed to understand its special value as an economic support for guerrilla war bases. He listened with attention when I expressed the opinion that a strong cooperative movement in China, if developed during the course of the war, could offer the best hope of an alternative to one-party rule and a renewed use of civil war as the only means of casting an opposition vote.

How, he wanted to know, could he help Indusco? I suggested that he
tell Chiang Kai-shek to earmark some of the American loans he was getting,
so that the cooperative organization could grow along with state and private
industry being financed by government credits. I wanted him, specifically
to ask Chiang to grant the twenty-million-yüan credit which Indusco was just
then demanding as a matter of urgent necessity to maintain its existing
units and to provide funds for expansion. The President thought that over
but decided he could not tell Chiang how to use our money, as he might
resent that. But he would, he said, express his keen personal interest in
Chinese Industrial Cooperatives, and ask for a report on their progress when
he next wrote to the Generalissimo.

"He will get the idea, I think," said F.D.R. When I saw him in 1944
Mr. Roosevelt reminded me of that promise. He said that he had carried it
out and had also asked Chiang and Mme Chiang about Indusco when he saw them
in Cairo. Indusco did for a while get some special credits and attention
from Chiang, though I have no idea whether that had any connection with my
talk with the President.

By 1944, following the dismissal of Stilwell, Roosevelt may already
have become too disillusioned with Chiang Kai-shek, and too puzzled and
discouraged by the outlook in Chinese internal affairs, to feel that his
personal intervention could any longer greatly influence matters. By 1945
he clearly recognized the growing strength of the Chinese Communists. In
that year he told me he was going to give them direct help in the conclud-
ing phase of the war against Japan. He had no apparent intention of
repudiating Chiang Kai-shek's regime; he may have regarded cooperation with
the Reds merely as a useful piece of military expediency. I got the impression also that Roosevelt may have conceived of the Reds as a means of
bringing pressure to bear on Chiang, to persuade him to move forward toward
modernizing his own government as the center of a united and progressive
China. I do not know whether he considered ultimate Communist victory a
serious possibility. He was certainly aware of the danger of a renewal of
civil war in the midst of the struggle against Japan.

"Over in Cairo," he said to me on May 26, 1944, "I told Chiang and
Mme Chiang that they had to do something to get together with the Reds.

I said that we were not going to get involved in any civil war situation over there, and that we wanted China united against Japan."

"If they don't work out some kind of coalition in the near future," I said, "there may be large-scale civil war even before Japan is defeated, or soon afterward."

"I'm inclined to agree, " he replied. He already saw it as a definite responsibility of American policy to bring about a compromise between the two camps. "Off the record I will tell you," he went on, "that two and a half months ago Chiang did agree to let us send some of our people to Yenan and let them stay there. Some kind of hitch developed and the Generalissimo asked us to wait a few weeks. Now I'm interested to see that Chiang has agreed to let the correspondents into Yenan. Off the record, too, we're sending somebody (for the government) with them, and he will probably stay there afterward."

When I saw the President on March 3, 1945 he had just heard about a breakdown in the negotiations General Patrick Hurley was conducting between Yenan and Chungking. It was "very disappointing news"--after earlier reports that a formula had been worked out satisfactorily. The President said Chiang Kai-shek had "raised some perfectly absurd objections" to Yenan's requests for certain guarantees of a rudimentary bill of rights. The latter appeared "perfectly reasonable" to him.

Roosevelt asked what I thought of Chiang personally, and whether I "liked" him or felt I "understood" him. I replied along lines I had already written in The Battle for Asia--not very flattering, I fear. As to whether I "liked" him, I had interviewed him several times but had not changed my opinion. He said:

"I never was able to form any opinion of Chiang at Cairo. When I thought about it later I realized that all I knew was what Mme Chiang told me about her husband and what he thought. She was always there to phrase all the answers. I got to know her, but this fellow Chiang--I never could break through to him at all. I'm hoping Pat Hurley will be able to tell me a little more when he gets back."

"We spoke further of the Chinese Communists and whether they were aiming at a proletarian dictatorship--whether they were "real Communists"

or, as some people then claimed, "only agrarian reformers." I repeated what
I had said earlier and had often written, that their immediate program was
agrarian reform--or agrarian equalitarianism--but that they were Marxists
and their goal was communism. Their ties with Moscow in recent years had
been largely ideological; they had received no military aid from Russia
for a decade. Of course they were members of the Comintern. Had the
Comintern really been dissolved? It was a question open to speculation how
closely Moscow could or would control them in the future. One way to find
out might be to establish closer ties with them in the common war against
Japan.

The President asked a few questions about what, concretely, the Eighth
Route (Red) Army could do with our aid. He then said we were actually planning to land supplies and liaison officers on the north China coast. Thereto-
fore, I knew, we had given no help to the Chinese Communist forces. Naturally I assumed that in the North China operation we would try to find
Kuomintang-led guerrillas to work with. I wondered how the Reds, who by
then held effective control of most of North China beyond the cities and
roads patrolled by the Japanese, would react to that.

"I suppose," I said, "that as long as we recognize Chiang as the sole
government we must go on sending all supplies exclusively through him (even
when dealing with guerrillas)? We can't support two governments in China,
can we?"

"Well, I've been working with two governments there," the President
responded, throwing back his head emphatically, "and I intend to go on doing
so until we get them together."

The Marine Raiders seemed tailor-made for the North China project.
Their leader, Evans Carlson, was one of the few American officers respected
by Kuomintang and Communist commanders alike. F.D.R. had known Carlson
since he had commanded his presidential bodyguard at Quantico, where they
became friends. White House backing had been essential to overcome the old-
line Marine opposition to the whole Raider training system which Carlson had
set up--one of the most original ideas in combat indoctrination introduced
by our armed services during World War II. Jimmy Roosevelt had been Carlson's
executive officer, and he later became commander of the Second Raider Battalion.

"Jimmy," his father once said to me, "is crazy about Carlson."

I spoke of Carlson now; I had just returned from California, where I had visited him. He was then convalescing from wounds sustained in Saipan. The President was relieved to hear that he was well enough to be reassigned. Carlson, he agreed, was obviously best suited for the work in North China. He had, he said, already suggested his name. "But the Marine brass won't hear of it," Roosevelt snorted. "Say he's too much of a Red!"

I said Evans Carlson was no Communist. (He was one of those people whom Dostoyevsky's policeman called "far more dreadful"--a Christian who believed in God and also believed in socialism.) "He's about as much a Communist," I said, "as his New England preacher-father!"

"That's what I kept saying to the brass, but they can't see the difference!" F.D.R. smiled scornfully. "I told them to find somebody as good as Carlson, but they haven't had any luck so far."

It was then five months since the Generalissimo had won his personal victory by forcing Roosevelt to withdraw General Stilwell rather than give him authority to reorganize and retrain the Kuomintang armies and assume full command as Chiang's first deputy in order to impose other minimum reforms needed to save his regime from complete disintegration. The Generalissimo had had his way, but at the expense of bringing to the President's close scrutiny the most noisome details of inner corruption, demoralization and incompetence of Chiang's military, economic and political household. Soon afterward Roosevelt went to Yalta. Who could doubt that his attitude there toward the disposition made of Manchuria was at least somewhat determined by the Generalissimo's stubborn rejection of the President's and General Marshall's choice of Stilwell as the man best suited to accomplish the arduous and complex task of "saving China"?

What a difference it might have made in the Generalissimo's fate if he had given Stilwell command and thus had been able to hold him--and through him the United States--responsible for restoring Manchuria to the Kuomintang, intact, after the war! Most of the terms which governed Russia's entry into the conflict against Japan might have been accepted by Roosevelt even if Stiwell had not been dismissed, but the end results might have then been vastly better for Chiang Kai-shek.

Just what did Roosevelt foresee as the possible future of our relations with the Chinese Communists? What did he mean when, fresh from Yalta and with the still secret terms of his agreement with Russia lying newly minted on his consciousness if not his conscience, he said to me, "I'm working with two governments (in China) and I intend to go on doing so . . . . "? Did he regard the presence of our diplomatic and military observers in Yenan as a kind of de facto recognition of the separate Communist power there--or as a wartime earnest of American aid against Japan?

Roosevelt died the next month. Soon afterward all talk of a North China landing or any serious military collaboration with Yenan abruptly ended, as all our support was thrown behind Chiang Kai-shek and the big gamble on the survival of one-man rule. That closed the chapter on our chance to find out how the Chinese Communists would behave toward us--and toward Russia--if treated as our ally in the common war against Japan, as happened in the case of the Yugoslavian Communists in the joint war against Hitler.

APPENDIX

BIOGRAPHIES IN BRIEF

Recorded in late August and
early September, 1936, in Kansu

CH'IEN TSUNG-HSIN 錢宗信 , director public health bureau of the Fifteenth
Army Corps. Ch'ien was born in Wusung, Kiangsu, in 1911, and was educated
in Wusung schools. In 1925 he entered T'ing-chi University, Wusung, to
study engineering. A year later he had to leave because of lack of funds.
Then he worked in the Paulun Hospital for five years as a nurse (Burkill
Road, Shanghai). He left there to join the Kuomintang Tenth Division in
1931 as a hospital director. Having enlisted for patriotic reasons during
the Shanghai war, he soon afterward found himself shifted to the anti-Red
war. Dissatisfied, he deserted and sought out the Reds. At first the
Communists thought he was a spy and imprisoned him. In 1933 he was released
and began to work in the Red Army General Hospital. Then he was assigned
as director of hospital work in the Twenty-fifth Army, in the E-yü-wan
soviet district. After the base there was abandoned he came to Shensi, to
his present post, where he is one of three "doctors" in the field hospital
service. When he joined the Reds he was twenty. He was angry over the non-
resistance policy in Manchuria. He is now a convinced Marxist.

CHU JUI 朱瑞 , chairman of the political training department, First Army
Corps, a native of Kiangsu from a landlord family, was born in 1905 and
went through middle school in Nanking and then studied in the Eastern
Toilers University in the Soviet Union. Later he attended the Red Army
Academy in the U.S.S.R. He was in Russia from 1926 to 1930, and in 1928
joined the Communist party, having before that been a Young Communist. On
his return from Russia he worked in Shanghai and Hankow and then went with
Nieh Jung-chen to Kiangsu. He is unmarried. He had not seen anybody from
his immediate family for eleven years.

HSIAO HUA 蕭華 , born in Hsin-kuo-hsien, Kiangsi, in 1914, is the son of
a peasant family. He joined the Reds at the age of fourteen at Chingkangshan.
Entirely educated by the Communists and the Red Army, he was in 1936 deputy

political commissar of the Second Division, First Army Corps.

HSÜ HSIANG-CH'IEN 徐向前 , commander of the Fourth Front Red Army. As
told to Edgar Snow by General Ch'en Keng.

Hsü was born in Shansi. He was a Whampoa student in the first class
with Ch'en Keng. After graduating he worked for Yang Hu-ch'eng. During the
Great Revolution he went to Canton and there participated in the Communist
uprising. At that time he joined the party. Following the failure in Canton
he went to the Hailufeng soviet, where the first Communist government was
set up and was soon destroyed. Then he worked in Shanghai till about 1930.
At that time he entered the Hupeh-Hunan-Anhui guerrilla area and became
commander of the Tenth Division. Later he was promoted to commander of the
Fourth Army, then the Fourth Front Army.

In 1931, during the war with Ch'en T'iao-yuan 陳調元, Hsü destroyed
four divisions and two brigades, captured three brigade commanders, and one
commander in chief. The Reds took a total of 15,000 rifles.

Ch'en greatly admires Hsü as a commander. He has organized many skill-
ful campaigns in their entirety. When he went to Szechwan he had thirty to
forty thousand men with him, an army created in three or four years. The
First Army Corps (Kiangsi) was superior in tactical training (Ch'en said)
but the Fourth Army had the most power, was obstinate, determined and full
of strong fighting spirit.

LI FU-CH'UN 李富春 , chairman of the Central Committee of Shensi-Kansu-
Ninghsia Communist party (August 1936).

Li was born in 1899 near Changsha, Hunan. His father was a teacher
in a boy's school. Three brothers, one older and two younger, have remained
in the White areas, as has the rest of his family.

Li studied at Changsha at the same time Mao, Lo Man (Li Wei-han 李維
漢) and Ts'ai Ho-sheng were students there. He was recruited with other
students and workers from Hunan in the work-and-study corps (work three
months, study three months) organized to go to France in World War I. He
became an "adjuster" in a motor factory in Paris and Lyons. He also worked
in the Schneider munitions plant, and there he met French Communists who

talked to him and gave him books and papers to read, such as L'Humanité.
He arrived in France in 1919 and joined the Communist party of France in
1921. He married Ts'ai Ch'ang there. Soon afterward a branch of the
Communist party of China was organized in France and Li joined that; he
was one of the five members of the central committee at the beginning.
Chou En-lai was another.

From France Li went to the U.S.S.R. and studied for half a year in
the Eastern Toilers University. In 1925 he returned to China and worked
in the Second Army under T'an Yen-k'ai, where he was a political worker
(with the Kuomintang forces) until 1927. After the counter-revolution he
went to Hupeh and worked in the Left-wing Kuomintang armies there. Following the collapse of the Wuhan government he fled to Shanghai and worked
underground on the military committee until 1931, when it was liquidated
temporarily. He fled to Hongkong but returned again in the same year to
represent Chou En-lai on the military advisory committee. Chou had gone
to the Soviet Union.

In 1932 Li entered Kiangsi to work in the Red Army political department, at first; then he joined the provincial party central committee.
During the Long March he was with the political department of the Red Army.
Upon arrival in the Northwest he assumed his present post, in 1935. He
speaks French and knows some English and Russian.

LIU CH'ANG-HAN 劉昌漢 , chairman of the revolutionary committee, Ninghsia
province, headquarters at Yu-wang-hsien, was born in Wa-yao-pao, Shensi, in
1913. He studied in the primary schools there. His family was very poor;
he left school to support his parents. In 1927 a school teacher introduced
him to the party and helped him. He went back to school and remained there
till 1932. During these years he organized a Communist group in the school.
After he graduated in 1932 he was sent to work in the hsien (Yu-wang-hsien)
and in the army. By this time his family was completely bankrupt. They had
not even a cave and lived with relatives in their cave. Partisan warfare
now spread to Anting. The Twenty-seventh and Twenty-eighth Red Armies were
formed, under Hsieh Tzu-chia 謝子嘉 , and the Twenty-sixth Army under
Liu Chih-tan.

NIEH HO-T'ING 聶鶴亭 . Recorded during an interview at Yu-wang-hsien, Kansu, August 28, 1936.

Nieh was chief of staff of the First Front Red Army at this time. He was born in Fuyang (Hu-yuan), Anhui, in 1908. His family had been small landlords during his grandfather's time. When he was born they had forty mou of land but owed others seven to eight hundred dollars; they were thus "middle peasants." He began primary school at the age of seven, and entered Han-Mei Middle School of Hu-yuan, Anhui, a missionary school, at the age of fourteen. A year later he entered normal school at Anching, capital of Anhui. Two years later he graduated. While in middle school he was a member of the student government and a tai-piao (delegate) to student conferences.

In middle school he first heard of communism. Members of the party there influenced him. He read ABC of Communism and The Leader, a Left magazine. When he joined the student government there was a movement against Ts'ao K'un 曹錕 and his corrupt regime in Peking. Students of Anching surrounded the tu-chun's yamen and demonstrated; his guards killed two students. An order was issued for Nieh's arrest and he fled to Nanchang. There he enrolled in a military academy run by General Fang Wen-pen. After six months in the academy he went to Shanghai to establish contact with the Communist party, to whose headquarters he was introduced by a schoolmate. He was given work to do by General Kao Yu-hui. He joined the party and was sent to Anching to agitate among students and organize them. While there, he taught in a private middle school for a year and a half. There were three Communists and ten Kuomintang members in Anching; together they organized support for the National Revolution.

In 1926 he left the school and returned to Shanghai. The Northern Expedition (of the Nationalist Revolution) had already begun. Nieh was sent back to Anhui, to the town of Ho-fei. The encirclement of Wuhan had begun. Nanchang had already fallen. The hinterland was a political vacuum. In accordance with his orders Nieh established connections with a middle-school teacher, who introduced him to a min-t'uan (militia) group in western Anhui. They were led by a Japanese-educated leftist student whose father was a local landlord; through him Nieh made connections with the hsien guards at Ho-fei. The min-t'uan had about 110 rifles, the hsien guards about 100.

In August they staged an uprising and raised the Kuomintang banner over the town. But because they lacked experience and failed to educate, discipline and reorganize the soldiers, they did not know how to develop relations with the people and win popular support.

On the third day after the uprising a battalion of provincial troops arrived at Ho-fei and defeated them. Their forces evaporated and Nieh and his Shanghai comrade fled westward.

Next day Nieh went on to Shanghai and re-established connections with the party. He was ordered to proceed to Wuhan and help organize the fifth column in the city, against the northern generals. He stopped off at Ho-fei and picked up fourteen students. They arrived at Wuhan after Wuchang (one of the three cities of Wuhan) had already fallen. They joined a party school and received special instruction on infiltration techniques. Nieh was soon assigned to work in Yeh T'ing's independent regiment, as a platoon commander. Party organization in Yeh T'ing's command was excellent and discipline was good; the regiment was inspected by Mme Sun, Borodin and General Bluecher, and was commended.

About this time the Shu-ko-shang (Hunan) mutiny occurred and Yeh T'ing's forces were called upon to participate. Yeh commanded a division and a regiment then and in one decisive battle smashed the forces of the Hunan warlord Hsia Tou-yin 夏斗寅 。 Soon after this Chiang Kai-shek turned counter-revolutionary, and before long the Wuhan government also turned against the Communists. Nieh was a company commander in Yeh T'ing's division when Yeh was transferred to Kiangsi, where he participated in the Nanchang uprising. With the help of General Chu Teh's police and the support of the Twenty-fourth and Twenty-fifth Kuomintang divisions the Communists seized that city in 1927. Following their defeat, Nieh joined the Red forces in the retreat to Hailufeng. Later they fled to south Kiangsi, where Chu Teh became commander in chief, Lin Piao commander, Yeh T'ing vice-commander, and Nieh political commissar, of the "first detachment" of the Communist revolutionary army--the remnants of the Nanchang uprising.

From Kiangsi Nieh was sent to report to the party in Shanghai. Then he proceeded to Canton, where he joined Chang Fa-k'uei's Fourth Army. His assignment was to organize communist cells in Chang's army to join the

Canton Uprising. He did succeed in taking a detachment of Chang's forces with him at that time. After the Canton Commune disaster Nieh fled into the interior with other survivors. Eventually he made his way back to Shanghai, where he did party work for nearly three years.

In the winter of 1929-30 Nieh was sent to the Kiangsi-Hunan soviet districts, where he became a divisional commander. During Chiang Kai-shek's Second Extermination Campaign, Nieh was wounded. When he recovered he became chief of staff of the Red Army's Eleventh Division. Later he was appointed chief of staff of the Twelfth Army. He participated in the second Communist attack on Changsha. He served throughout the wars against Chiang Kai-shek in South China and made the Long March--at which time he was a divisional commander. After the Red Army reached Kansu he was assigned to the commander in chief's staff. During the Shansi expedition (1935) he served as chief of the Red Army Politburo. Following that he became chief of staff of the First Front Army under General P'eng Teh-huai.

NIEH JUNG-CHEN 聶榮臻 , political commissar, First Army Corps, chief of staff, First Army Corps.

Nieh was born near Chungking, Szechwan, in 1899. He studied in middle school in Chungking and participated in the May Fourth Movement there. In 1920 he left for France as a worker-student. In Europe he studied natural science and French.

In France his ideas were at first nebulous. He wanted to work for the independence and modernization of China. He had been influenced by Ch'en Tu-hsiu and New Youth, but he did not know how to go beyond there. After a year in Paris he got a job in the Schneider plant, where he worked for a few months. Then he went to Belgium to Charles Roens (?). He studied in a workers college and acquired some technical training as an engineer and electrician. He was there almost two years before he returned to France and took a job as an electrical worker. He began to read Marxist literature in French; first, the Communist Manifesto, next an outline of Das Kapital. He read many other Marxist books; the same Frenchman who taught him French also taught him Marxism. Li Fu-ch'un had the same experience--with the same teacher.

In 1923 Nieh went to Berlin in a Red group with Li Fu-ch'un; he had meanwhile joined the Communist party. While he was in Germany he worked at organizing students. He was much impressed by the German party and had a good social life among the German comrades.

In 1924 he went on to Moscow where he studied six months at the Eastern Toilers University. Then he entered the Red Army Academy for a year. In 1925 he returned to China and entered Whampoa Academy, where he became a secretary in the political department, which office he held till March 21, 1926. At that time Chiang staged his first coup d'état. Nieh left the school and worked in the military committee of the party at Canton. Then he went to Shanghai to work with the party there. He joined the Kuomintang armies in Hunan and Hupeh--after the Shanghai counter-revolution. When the united front at Wuhan collapsed Nieh went to Nanchang, where he participated in the 1927 uprising. He was political commissar of Yeh T'ing's division.

After the defeat he went to Canton and took part in the ill-fated Canton insurrection. He fled to Hongkong with Yeh T'ing, and remained there till 1930, after which he went to Hopei to work with the military committee in Tientsin. In 1931 he returned to Shanghai as a member of the Central Committee's military advisory committee. The same year he went to Kiangsi and became vice-chairman of the political department of the Red Army.

From the time of its organization till now (1936) Nieh has been political commissar of the First Army Corps.

Nieh speaks German and some English, as well as French.

TENG HSIAO-P'ING 鄧 小 平 , deputy political commissar, First Army Corps. An autobiographical statement given to Edgar Snow at Yu-wan-pao, Kansu, August 19, 1936.

"I was born in Szechwan in 1896. In 1920 I went to France and stayed there for five years, as a worker. I did not attend school in France but in 1926 I went to Russia and studied there for several months. I returned to China during the Great Revolution and joined the Kuominchun at Ch'ang-an. After the counter-revolution in 1927 I did party work in Shanghai until 1929, when I joined the Seventh Red Army in Lungchow, Kwangsi.

"The Lungchow soviet had relations with the Annamite rebels who began the worker-peasant rebellion in 1930. French airplanes bombed Lungchow and we shot one down. After 1930 the Lungchow soviet was abandoned when the Seventh Red Army retreated to Kiangsi. From that time till now I have been doing party work in Kiangsi."

TENG HUA 鄧華 , born in Hunan in 1910, was in 1936 chairman of the political department of the Second Division, the oldest division of the Red Army. He came from a peasant family. He has been in the Red Army since he joined Mao Tse-tung at Chingkanshan. Most of his schooling was acquired in the Red Army, where he learned everything he knows about military science.

TS'AI CH'ANG 蔡暢 , head of the "White Area Work" and "Women's Work" of the party in the front areas (August 1936), was the only woman member of the Central Committee at the front. She was one of thirty veteran Communist women who completed the Long March.

Ts'ai Ch'ang and Teng Ying-ch'ao (Mrs. Chou En-lai) were perhaps the best educated of the older Communist women. Ts'ai's family had been prominent in Hunan; her grandfather was a Ch'ing scholar and official. She received a classical education to a degree unusual for girls. In 1919 she ran away from home and joined a group of "work-and-study" students who went to France. She met her husband there--Li Fu-ch'un, at present chairman of the Kansu-Ninghsia border soviet. They returned from France in 1923, both having meanwhile joined the branch Chinese Communist Party in France, with Chou En-lai.

Ts'ai Ch'ang participated in the Great Revolution and held posts in the Hankow government. She fled to Russia after the counter-revolution and studied there till 1932. Returning to China she got into Kiangsi and worked there until the defeat and the Long March. She attended the Ninth Congress of the Communist International in Moscow as a Chinese delegate in 1928.

Her brother, Ts'ai Ho-sen 蔡和森 , was an early radical leader in Hunan who influenced Mao Tse-tung. He organized, in Hunan, the Hsin-min Hsueh-hui 新民學會 , with Mao. He was arrested in Hongkong in 1931 and extradited to Canton, where he was executed.

Ts'ai has an attractive personality, speaks fluent French, and from the meagrest of materials, in impoverished Kansu, turned out meals that had all the aroma and flavor of dinner at Chambord's.

TSO CH'ÜAN 左權 , acting commander of the First Army Corps of the First Front Army, is of Hunanese peasant origin. He was born in 1906. In 1923 he joined the Kuomintang and in 1925 joined the Communist party. Accepted at Whampoa Academy as a cadet, he was a member of Class I. During the Great Revolution he was promoted to battalion commander. Following the counter-revolution he escaped from China and went to Russia, where he studied in the Red Army Academy for four years. When he returned to China in 1930 he went to Kiangsi and became an officer of the Red Army.

Tso Ch'üan is modest, good-looking and greatly respected by Red generals. Characteristically, he spent hours telling me of the Red Army's experiences on the Long March but said nothing of his own career beyond the foregoing. He was in command of a main column of the Red Army during the Long March.

WANG MING 王明 (Ch'en Shao-yü 程紹禹), as told to Edgar Snow by Po Ku (Ch'in Pang-hsien) in Pao-an, July 1936.

Wang Ming was the son of rich peasants in Anhui. He joined the party about 1925. From then until 1927 he attended Sun Yat-sen University in Moscow. In the Wuhan period he returned to China and worked in the Central Committee. After the counter-revolution he returned to Moscow for two years. Back in Shanghai, in 1929, he headed the party Agitation-Propaganda Bureau. Following that he did agitation-propaganda work in the All-China Trade Union Federation. At the fourth plenary session of the Central Committee (July 1931) he was elected to membership in the Central Committee and the Politburo. Soon afterward he was sent to Moscow to represent the Central Committee of the Chinese Communist Party in Comintern headquarters.

Wang Ming's great achievment (said Po Ku) was the breaking of Li Li-san and discrediting of his line. Li controlled all party organizations in 1930, and only four out of forty members of the Central Committee in Shanghai dared oppose him. Led by Wang, the three others were Po Ku, Wang Chia-hsiang and Ho Chih-shu, who was later captured and killed in the Hopei "model prison."

Wang has remained in Moscow till now (1936). He is married to a Chinese Communist, Meng Ch'ing-shu 孟慶樹 . He graduated from middle school in Anhui.

WANG SHOU-TAO 王首道 , chief of the political department, Fifteenth
Corps, Chinese Red Army; Yu-wang-hsien, Kansu, August 29, 1936.

Wang Shou-tao was born in Liu-yang, Hunan, and is now twenty-nine. His
family were poor peasants. He entered a primary school when he was nine,
where students had to buy only their own food, clothing and books. He did
well; he liked and was liked by his teachers. Once he asked a teacher to
draw a picture for him but when it was done a landlord's son asked for it
and the teacher gave it to him. Wang fought with the student but the
teacher punished him for doing so. He was much embittered by that experience and never forgot it. He had to cut wood to pay for his food and the
only wooded places were owned by landlords. He and his brother simply stole
the wood; they "had no other way." One day they were caught; his brother
was imprisoned by the landlord. He felt depressed and hopeless; "there was
no way out for the poor."

When Wang was twelve his family moved to a distant place and Wang was
left behind to live with his mother's brother. This uncle sent him to
become an apprentice under a firecracker-maker, but after half a year his
uncle relented and put him back in school, only this time with an old-
style Chinese teacher, whose name was Li. He studied under Li for a year;
then Li helped him enter a higher primary school. He was there after the
May Fourth Movement occurred; influenced by it he organized students into
a brotherhood. With several friends he agitated for a night school, for
mass education, against the Twenty-one Demands, etc. He also took part
in an amateur dramatic club to present modern plays.

He was now fourteen. At this time his father returned to the scene and
told him to get ready for his wedding. His father had betrothed him when he
was a child; he now had to see that Shou-tao fulfilled the bargain. But
Shou-tao had by now realized the wrong-headedness of arranged matches and
adolescent marriages; he had played the part of a girl "victim" in a play
about such a marriage. He refused and quarreled with his father. Eventually the match was broken off. When he was eighteen he entered Changsha
Shu-yüeh Middle School, with the help of some relatives. But he never had
enough to pay for his food and was always hungry. He borrowed money as
long as possible. Then he fasted. One night, weak from hunger, he broke

into the school restaurant and stole some food. He was discovered in the
act by the manager. While he waited for punishment he wrote an essay in
his notebook contrasting the impoverished students with the wealthy students
who were generally idle. A teacher came across this by chance, and as a
result took an interest in Wang. He helped him through the next term, and
then encouraged him to enter a state agricultural school, where tuition was
very low, only eight dollars per year.

Two years later the anti-Japanese movement reached Changsha. In 1924
Wang took part in agitation in the school and became a Young Communist. He
wrote a manifesto attacking the school government and authorities and was
expelled. Then he returned to Liu-yang, his home. There he read Ch'en
Tu-hsiu's New Youth. An article which described the peasants associations
in Canton inspired Wang to organize peasant groups in Hunan. By then he
"understood the nature of the class struggle." As he propagandized the
peasants the landlords complained and the government ordered his arrest.
He fled to Canton. On the way he stopped off in Shanghai. There, unknow-
ingly, he used a counterfeit silver dollar; he was arrested for this by
the British police. He was innocent, but the police treated him roughly and
fined him five dollars, which made quite a dent in his small capital, all
borrowed from friends.

In Canton Wang entered the peasant school organized by Mao Tse-tung.
P'eng Pai also taught there. In 1925 he joined the Communist party in
Canton. After receiving further Marxist instruction and learning some
fundamental principles of the land revolution from Mao, he returned to
Hunan. In Changsha he joined the Kuomintang, under the system of dual
party membership then sanctioned.

By 1926 he was in southern Hunan organizing peasants in the district
of Chi-yang. When the Shu-ko-shang mutiny occurred Wang escaped from
Chi-yang and fled to Tung-hu in southernmost Hunan, where he was hidden
by a peasant family for nearly five months. In this period he read the
Communist Manifesto and a condensation of Das Kapital. In the winter of
1927 he returned to his native town, Liu-yang, and led an uprising
there, as secretary of the Liu-yang-hsien party committee. Peasants under
him attempted to capture the walled hsien, or county seat. Their first
assault was begun with only one pistol and twenty men. They were repulsed.

Wang organized the peasants to carry through confiscation of land and
distribution of property to the poor. They then found widespread support
and extended their work to several districts.

In 1929 Wang was appointed secretary of the special party committee
for the Hunan-Kiangsi-Hupeh "border areas." He was twenty-two. The next
year General P'eng Teh-huai took Changsha and he became P'eng's "secretary
of political activities." Later he became chairman of the first Hunan
provincial soviet. Li Li-san was nominal chairman but he never reached the
interior. Wang's wife went to Changsha to organize textile workers. She
was discovered and executed by General Ho Chien 何鍵 , Kuomintang
governor of Hunan. Wang was pursued but escaped and finally reached Shanghai.
There he did party work till 1932 when he returned to the Hunan-Kiangsi Red
areas, working as a party functionary. Ho Chien had recovered the walled
towns, but after two years the villages were still pro-Red. When hsien
police went to the countryside to collect taxes the peasants beat them and
drove them away. The landlords could collect no rents.

When Hsiao K'e became commander of the Sixth Red Army Corps in 1933
Wang went with him. The next year Wang attended the Second All-Soviet
Congress. Then he made the Long March with the Red Army to the Northwest.
During the Shansi expedition he was on the military committee of the Red
Army Staff. At the end of that campaign he became head of the political
department of the Fifteenth Army Crops.

Wang was an active political worker in Kiangsi and Hunan during the
period when the Reds attempted collectivization on a small scale. "The
results were not good," he said. "We attempted to consolidate all farms
and to divide the work and the product among all peasants more or less
equally. The peasants did not respond to this. Their demand was for land
of their own to cultivate, on the basis of each family for itself. After
some failures the party recognized this and altered its policy."

Wang thinks collectivization may be possible in the future but is not
necessary at present. "When the Soviet is in power over several provinces
or a great part of China and its power is adequate, then collectivization
can be undertaken with energy and confidence and moderation," he said.

YANG CHIH-CH'ENG 楊至誠 , party secretary of the First Front Army front
area, headquarters at Ho-lien-wan. Yang is (1936) 38. He was born in
Kweichow, near the Hunan border. His father and mother were "small landlords"
and he was sent to old-style schools for six years. After that he joined a
tu-chün army in Szechwan, under General Hsin Kai-wan. Just before the
Great Revolution he joined the Kuomintang and was sent to Whampoa Academy,
where he studied under Borodin and Chiang Kai-shek. He was assigned to
Ho Lung's Twentieth Army during the Northern Expedition. He joined the
Communist party at this time, and participated in the Nanchang Uprising.

Yang retreated with Chu Teh, Ho Lung and Lin Piao to Amoy, where the
Communists were also defeated, and next fled to south Kiangsi with Chu Teh.
He was present when (in 1928) Chu Teh and Mao Tse-tung joined forces at
Chingkanshan. He has been with the Red Army ever since, making the Long
March via Szechwan and Kansu. During the Reds' (1935) expedition to Shansi
he was a member of the field staff. He is a specialist in military adminis-
tration and base organization problems. A quick-talking, efficient, active
man, he seems shrewd and intelligent. In addition to being party chief of
the district, he is head of communications. He remarked that he had not
seen a movie or play for nine years. He asked me to send him books and
papers--anything to read. He had not seen a copy of Inprecorr for four
years.

YANG TEH-CHIH 楊德志 , born in Hunan in 1910 of peasant origin, studied
at Red Army Academy in Kiangsi. He was in 1936 deputy commander (at twenty-
six) of the Second Division.

GENERAL YEH CHIEN-YING 葉劍英 , as told to Edgar Snow at Pao-an, July
1936.

Yeh was born in Canton in 1903, in a merchant family. He studied in
Cantonese primary school and from there went to Yunnanfu, then a revolutionary
center of China. T'ang Chi-yao was governor; he had participated in the
overthrow of Yuan Shih-k'ai. Yeh graduated in the twelfth class of the
Yunnan Military Academy--six years behind Chu Teh, who had been a graduate
of the first class. From Yunnanfu Yeh went to Fukien, where he joined the

army of Ch'en Ch'i-mei under whom Chiang Kai-shek also served. Ch'en was the uncle of Ch'en Li-fu and Ch'en Kuo-fu 陳果夫 , later bosses of the Kuomintang, and he was said to have sponsored Chiang Kai-shek as a member of the secret society, the Ch'ing Pang. Chiang Kai-shek was Yeh's fellow officer in Ch'en's Fukien army.

Ch'en sent Yeh to Canton, to work with Sun Yat-sen and the Kuomintang. After the Sun-Joffe agreement, which provided for Russian aid to the Kuomintang, and two-party cooperation, Yeh joined the Communist party. He became an instructor at Whampoa, under Galens (Bluecher), and remained there until the launching of the Northern Expedition in 1926. He commanded the Twenty-first Division, one of three (First, Second, Twenty-first) under Chiang Kai-shek's personal command. (Chou En-lai said that Yeh left in "disgust" after Chiang's disastrous attack on Nanchang, early in 1927, but it seems likely he may have fled in advance of the coming purge.) He participated in the Canton Uprising (Kuantung pao-tung) and in the Canton Commune (Kuantung kung-she). After the suppression of the Commune he fled to Hongkong, then to Shanghai. In 1929 he went to Moscow, where he studied for two years. Returning to Shanghai he went to Kiangsi almost at once, and assumed important staff responsibilities. He is at present chief of the General Staff of the Eastern Front and a member of the Revolutionary Military Council. He speaks Russian, German, and a little bit of English. He is unmarried.

> After the Sian Incident Yeh went to Nanking, Hankow and Chungking with Chou En-lai, as part of the Reds' liaison team. In this role he became acquainted with many foreign newsmen and diplomats. Chou was basically a political general and relied heavily on Yeh's military knowledge and ability to analyze military situations. He was highly regarded for his sound strategic concepts by both Mao and Chou.

INDEX, AND NAMES IN CHINESE

Note: While most persons referred to in the text are easily identifiable, there are some who were and have remained inconspicuous in history. It would seem invidious, however, to try to distinguish here between well-known and inconspicuous persons. We have therefore inserted a full list, except in certain cases where persons were so very inconspicuous that neither the author nor other sources have been able to provide the characters for their names.

HARVARD EAST ASIAN MONOGRAPHS

1. Liang Fang-chung, *The Single-Whip Method of Taxation in China*

2. Harold C. Hinton, *The Grain Tribute System of China, 1845-1911*

3. Ellsworth C. Carlson, *The Kaiping Mines, 1877-1912*

4. Chao Kuo-chün, *Agrarian Policies of Mainland China: A Documentary Study, 1949-1956*

5. Edgar Snow, *Random Notes on Red China, 1936-1945*

6. Edwin George Beal, Jr., *The Origin of Likin, 1835-1864*

7. Chao Kuo-chün, *Economic Planning and Organization in Mainland China: A Documentary Study, 1949-1957*

8. John K. Fairbank, *Ch'ing Documents: An Introductory Syllabus*

9. Helen Yin and Yi-chang Yin, *Economic Statistics of Mainland China, 1949-1957*

10. Wolfgang Franke, *The Reform and Abolition of the Traditional Chinese Examination System*

11. Albert Feuerwerker and S. Cheng, *Chinese Communist Studies of Modern Chinese History*

12. C. John Stanley, *Late Ch'ing Finance: Hu Kuang-yung as an Innovator*

13. S.M. Meng, *The Tsungli Yamen: Its Organization and Functions*

14. Ssu-yü Teng, *Historiography of the Taiping Rebellion*

15. Chun-Jo Liu, *Controversies in Modern Chinese Intellectual History: An Analytic Bibliography of Periodical Articles, Mainly of the May Fourth and Post-May Fourth Era*

16. Edward J.M. Rhoads, *The Chinese Red Army, 1927-1963: An Annotated Bibliography*

17. Andrew J. Nathan, *A History of the China International Famine Relief Commission*

34. Ying-wan Cheng, *Postal Communication in China and Its Modernization, 1860-1896*

35. Tuvia Blumenthal, *Saving in Postwar Japan*

36. Peter Frost, *The Bakumatsu Currency Crisis*

37. Stephen C. Lockwood, *Augustine Heard and Company, 1858-1862: American Merchants in China*

38. Robert R. Campbell, *James Duncan Campbell: A Memoir by His Son*

39. Jerome Alan Cohen, ed., *The Dynamics of China's Foreign Relations*

40. V.V. Vishnyakova-Akimova, *Two Years in Revolutionary China, 1925-1927*, tr. Steven I. Levine

41. Meron Medzini, *French Policy in Japan during the Closing Years of the Tokugawa Regime*

42. *The Cultural Revolution in the Provinces*

43. Sidney A. Forsythe, *An American Missionary Community in China, 1895-1905*

44. Benjamin I. Schwartz, ed., *Reflections on the May Fourth Movement: A Symposium*

45. Ching Young Choe, *The Rule of the Taewŏn'gun, 1864-1873: Restoration in Yi Korea*

46. W.P.J. Hall, *A Bibliographical Guide to Japanese Research on the Chinese Economy, 1958-1970*

47. Jack J. Gerson, *Horatio Nelson Lay and Sino-British Relations, 1854-1864*

48. Paul Richard Bohr, *Famine and the Missionary: Timothy Richard as Relief Administrator and Advocate of National Reform*

49. Endymion Wilkinson, *The History of Imperial China: A Research Guide*

50. Britten Dean, *China and Great Britain: The Diplomacy of Commercial Relations, 1860-1864*

51.   Edward W. Wagner, *The Literati Purges: Political Conflict in Early Yi Korea*

52.   Yeh-chien Wang, *An Estimate of the Land-Tax Collection in China, 1753 and 1908*

53.   Richard M. Pfeffer, *Understanding Business Contracts in China, 1949-1963*